OCEANS
OF THE WORLD
OUR ESSENTIAL RESOURCE

Commercial research vehicles like this Perry "cubmarine" are used to survey oil drilling sites and inspect rig equipment once it's in place.

OCEANS
OF THE WORLD
OUR ESSENTIAL RESOURCE

BY KIRK POLKING

A GLOBAL PERSPECTIVES BOOK

PHILOMEL BOOKS
NEW YORK

The author and Philomel Books wish to thank the following individuals
and institutions whose photographs appear in this book:

Black Star, Frontispiece © 1978 Flip Schulke; p. 57 © 1978 Flip Schulke;
p. 67 © 1978 Kosti Ruohomaa; p. 81 © 1978 Sipa Press;
color section: Japanese man with kelp, Eiji Miyazawa;
sinking of the tanker, *Cadiz*, John Launois;
parrotfish in a coral reef, Jack Drake; female aquanaut, Flip Schulke
The Image Bank, jacket illustration by L.D. Gordon; color section:
California coastline, David Muench
FAO Photo and F. Mattioli, p. 72; color section: Senegalese fisherman
U.S. Library of Congress, p. 14
NOAA, p. 21
U.S. Naval Photographic Center, pp. 32, 33
Lockheed Missiles and Space Co., Inc., pp. 34, 42
The American Petroleum Institute, p. 45; color section: off-shore
loading platform, Gulf of Mexico; supertanker offloading cargo; "Guppy"
Kennecott Copper Corporation, p. 49
The Miami Seaquarium, p. 54
U.S. Navy Ocean Systems Center, p. 60
John Ryther, p. 69
B.P. Chemicals, p. 75
F.S. Hicks, p. 98
Kelco Communications, color section: otter
Scripps Institution of Oceanography, color section: FLIP
Woods Hole Oceanographic Institute, color section: *Alvin*
T.N. Wynne (The Oceanic Society), color section: students with otter trawl
Oceaneering International, Inc., color section: Jim diving suit

Maps and diagrams are by George Boctel

Published by Philomel Books, New York, 1983.
Philomel Books are published by The Putnam Publishing Group
51 Madison Avenue, New York, New York 10010
Printed in the United States of America.

Library of Congress Cataloging in Publication Data
Polking, Kirk. Oceans of the world.
Summary: Discusses the formation, geologic features,
life forms, uses, and future of the world's oceans.
I. Ocean—Juvenile literature. [1. Ocean] I. Title.
GC21.5.P64   551.46   82-357
ISBN 0-399-20919-0 AACR2

ACKNOWLEDGMENTS

The author gratefully acknowledges the time given by the following people for personal interviews in connection with this book:

At the Scripps Institution of Oceanography, La Jolla, California (interviews arranged by Jacqueline Parker, Director of Public Affairs): Dr. Angelo F. Carlucci, Marine Microbiology; Michael Guberek, Satellite Oceanography Facility; Dr. Osmund Holm-Hansen, Marine Biology; William A. Nierenberg, Director, Scripps; John D. Powell, Hydraulics Laboratory; Carl Sisskind, Deep Sea Drilling Project; Bud Smithey, Marine Biology; Dr. Richard C. J. Somerville, Experimental Long Range Forecast Center; Dr. A. Aristides Yayanos, Physiological Research Laboratory.

At the Woods Hole Oceanographic Institution, Woods Hole, Massachusetts (interviews arranged by Vicky Cullen, Publications and Information Manager): Dr. Richard Backus, Senior Scientist, Biology; Dr. Melbourne G. Briscoe, Physical Oceanography; Dr. Timothy J. Cowles, Biology; Dr. John Ewing, Chairman, Geology and Geophysics; Dr. Earl Hays, Chairman, Ocean Engineering; Dr. David Ross, Director, Marine Policy and Ocean Management; Dr. Geoffrey Thompson, Chairman, Chemistry; Val Worthington, Senior Scientist, Physical Oceanography.

Other scientists, institutions, and organizations that provided information, either through personal interview or by correspondence: Prof. Alan Bowmaker, Director, Oceanographic Research Institute, Durban, South Africa; Dr. Charles J. Brine, Forrestal Center Laboratory, FMC Corp.; Arnie Bryce, kelp-methane gas project, General Electric Company; Dr. E. T. Degens, Geologisch-Palaontologisches Institut, University of Hamburg; Food and Agriculture Organization of the United Nations; Donald L. Keach, Institute for Marine and Coastal Studies, University of Southern California; Ronald H. McPeak, Senior Marine Biologist, Kelco, Div. of Merck and Co., Inc.; David L. Meyer, Department of Geology, University of Cincinnati; Prof. A. S. Monin, Director, Institute of Oceanology, Moscow, USSR; National Oceanic and Atmospheric Administration; Naval Ocean Systems Center, San Diego; Dr. Michael Neushul, Dept. of Biological Sciences, University of California, Santa Barbara; Wheeler J. North, Environmental Sciences, California Institute of Technology; Ocean Research Institute, University of Tokyo; Marc I. Pinsel, U.S. Naval Oceanographic Office, Bay St. Louis, Mississippi; Elliot L. Richardson, former delegate to United Nations Law of the Sea Treaty Conference; John H. Ryther, Institute of Food and Agricultural Sciences, University of Florida; Dr. F. G. Walton Smith, The International Oceanographic Foundation; Dr. Barbara Sullivan, School of Oceanography, University of Rhode Island; David Swartz, Sea Grant Program, University of Maryland; James R. Taylor Jr., Food and Drug Administration; Dr. R. Eugene Turner, Center for Wetland Resources, Louisiana State University; Jean Yehle, Rosenstiel School of Marine and Atmospheric Science, University of Miami.

CONTENTS

1

THE WORLD OCEAN

What primeval urge draws us irresistibly to the sea? Is it because we are mostly water ourselves and perhaps came from the sea millions of years ago?

For centuries men and women have tried to unlock the secrets of the sea, and have savored the sense of adventure and freedom it offers. Sailors in flimsy craft set out to horizons for which no maps existed. Princes and potentates fought for dominion over watery kingdoms. Philosophers debated the origin of the oceans and how life emerged from this primordial soup.

And yet, strange as it may seem, we know less today about the seas that lie all around us than we do about the moon, which is some 238,000 miles away. In fact, when we first saw our planet through the eyes of an astronaut in space who photographed it, we marveled at the blueness of its surface. That continuous blue is the world ocean. Its four main parts in order of size are the Pacific, the Atlantic, the Indian, and the Arctic oceans. We sometimes use the word *sea* instead of ocean; but a sea can also be a smaller body of saltwater that is more or less surrounded by land, such as the

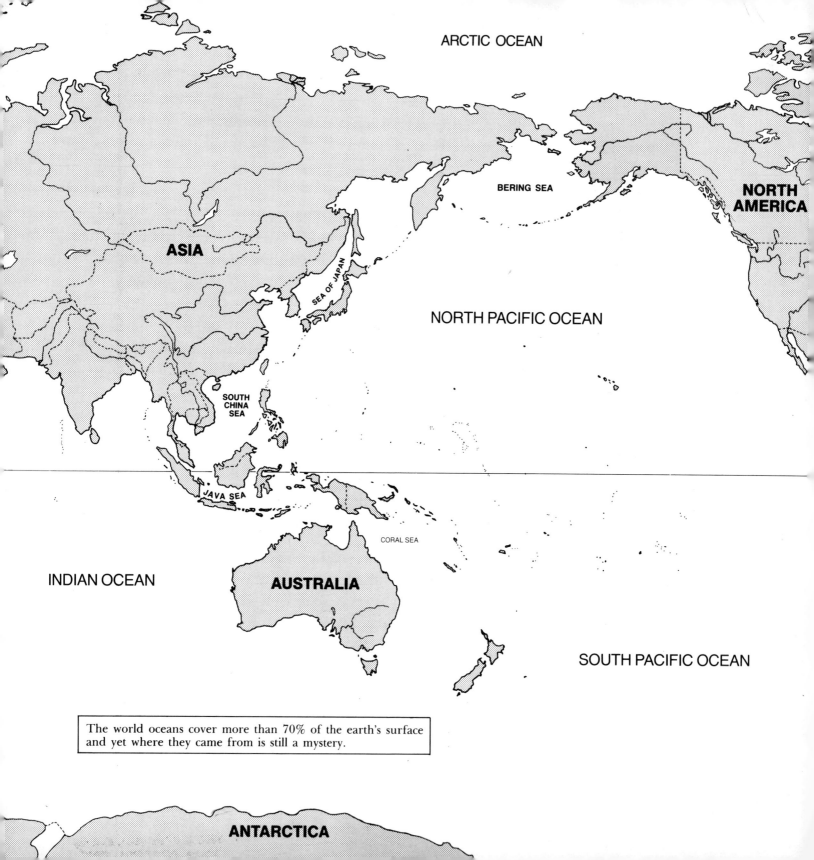

ARCTIC OCEAN

NORTH AMERICA

BERING SEA

ASIA

SEA OF JAPAN

NORTH PACIFIC OCEAN

SOUTH CHINA SEA

JAVA SEA

CORAL SEA

INDIAN OCEAN

AUSTRALIA

SOUTH PACIFIC OCEAN

The world oceans cover more than 70% of the earth's surface and yet where they came from is still a mystery.

ANTARCTICA

EUROPE

NORTH SEA

BALTIC SEA

CASPIAN SEA

BLACK SEA

MEDITERRANEAN SEA

NORTH ATLANTIC OCEAN

CARIBBEAN SEA

AFRICA

RED SEA

ARABIAN SEA

SOUTH AMERICA

SOUTH ATLANTIC OCEAN

Mediterranean; or an inland lake of saltwater such as the Dead Sea near Israel and the Caspian Sea between Iran and Russia.

We know many details about the great bodies of water that cover more than 70 percent of our globe. But there is one very important thing we don't know: where did the oceans come from? As far as we know, oceans don't exist on any other planet in our solar system. Only earth has a surface temperature in which water remains a liquid: between 32° F (0° C), the point at which water freezes, and 212° F (100° C), when it becomes a gas. All the other planets are either too hot or too cold.

Of course, scientists have many theories about how oceans were formed. Some think that billions of years ago, clouds of gases rose from the crust of the earth, which at that time was extremely hot. As the outer shell of the crust cooled, the vapor condensed, filling the depressions in the earth's surface with water. Others think that water has been added to the oceans slowly, over billions of years, from the heating of volcanic rock in the earth. These molten rocks contain small amounts of water, and when they reach the earth's surface, some is released.

If you look at a map of the world, you will see that the west coasts of Europe and Africa and the east coasts of North and South America fit together like two pieces of a jigsaw puzzle. From this fact, in 1912, the German meteorologist and explorer Alfred Wegener developed the idea that there was once an ancient, single continent, which he called Pangaea, and the other two-thirds of the world was one large ocean. Wegener theorized that Pangaea cracked and drifted apart about 135 million years ago, and when the continent parted, the Atlantic Ocean was formed.

More recently, two American geologists, Harry Hess and Robert Dietz, proposed another theory on how the continent separated. They believe that the crust of the earth underneath the Atlantic Ridge (now an undersea mountain range) cracked and was pulled apart. Lava from the molten layer underneath the crust flowed into the crack. When the lava cooled, since it is heavier than the surrounding continental rocks, gravity made it settle at a lower level. Seawater then flowed into the lower level. This cracking action continued over millions of years, and as the ocean floor spread apart, the continent separated.

Although we are still trying to learn how the oceans were formed, we do know a bit more about the movement of water in them. We have discovered, for example, that water moves vertically. Strong trade winds may move surface water away from coastlines, as they do near Peru, and cooler, deeper water will then rise to the surface. But the major vertical circulation in the ocean takes place when water on the surface becomes denser, through a combination of water temperature and salinity. Heavier water-masses sink and must be replaced by deeper water-masses rising to the surface.

We know of course that water is moved horizontally by the wind, and we have also discovered that there are large, constantly circulating surface-current systems in the oceans called gyres. The best-known of these gyres is made up of the northern equatorial current and the Gulf Stream. The Gulf Stream, one of many "rivers" on the surface of the ocean, is clearly visible in the Florida Straits. Although Spanish explorers knew about the Gulf Stream as early as the sixteenth century and rode its swift northeasterly current to speed up their voyages back to Spain, they kept their findings secret. It wasn't until 1770 that Benjamin Franklin made a chart showing the movement of the Gulf Stream. This chart was used by ships that carried the mail between England and America. Franklin, who made several sailings across the Atlantic and took surface seawater temperatures each day, found that his observations were the same as those of early American whalers: the Gulf Stream current was warmer than the ocean water on either side of

In the remarks accompanying his chart of the Gulf Stream, Benjamin Franklin warned westbound ship captains who tried to avoid the shoals around Nantucket that if they kept too far south, they could be slowed by the strong easterly current of the Stream.

it and must have flowed north from warmer climates.

While surface currents are created primarily by the prevailing winds of the hemisphere, there are also undersea streams created by the interaction of water temperature and salinity. The Mediterranean Sea is one of the saltiest on earth because it is surrounded by warm areas that create heavy evaporation of water. This dense, salty water sinks down and flows out through the deeper levels of the Strait of Gibraltar, as the passage between Spain and Africa connecting the Mediterranean and the Atlantic is called. At the same time, the warm surface water of the Atlantic flows into the Mediterranean, creating a powerful current. In the days when ships were propelled by sails, the force of the incoming currents was such that vessels were prevented from moving out into the Atlantic unless they had a wind strong enough to overcome the current. In fact, British Admiral Lord Nelson's victory over the French and Spanish fleet in 1805 was largely due to these currents. The enemy ships were delayed in the Mediterranean long enough for Nelson to deploy his ships outside the strait in a formation that enabled him to capture twenty enemy ships without losing a single one of his own. During World War II, submarine captains used these currents to slip in and out of the Mediterranean without using telltale engines.

Ocean currents also have an effect on land temperatures, as can be seen in the climates of California or Asia. We don't yet know as much as we'd like about the combination of sun, atmosphere, wind, and water that creates ocean currents, but we've mapped the movements of currents from the equator, the Arctic, and various parts of the ocean to show why, for example, warm water touches the shores of California and Japan. And, of course, warm surface water, in turn, affects the nearby land temperature.

We have discovered that oceans are important in determining the climate of the earth. The oceans absorb heat from the sun and

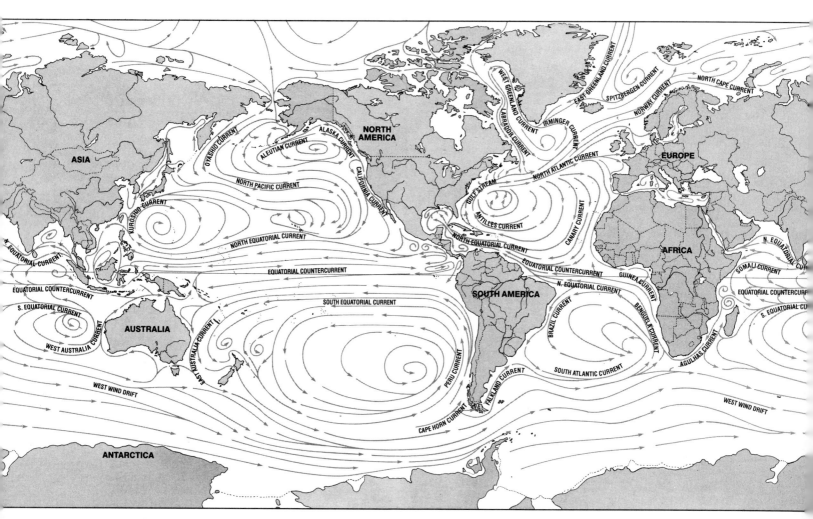

In addition to surface currents of the world oceans that are created by the wind and the earth's rotation, other currents also flow near the bottom of the sea.

then evaporate water from the sea surface. As the water evaporates, it leaves the salt behind and condenses into clouds that return fresh water to the earth in the form of either rain or snow. When cold air comes in contact with warm land or water, fog forms—a cloud of moisture-filled air close to the ground. Ocean currents transport heat from the equator toward the poles, and the earth's rotation and the action of the wind keep temperatures at levels that permit us to live almost everywhere on earth.

Although we tend to think of each ocean as a single large body of water, there are also oceans within oceans—the world ocean is, in fact, made up of many separate masses of water, each defined by its characteristics of temperature and salt content. The consistent, scientific study of deep ocean waters did not start until the 1950s, but since then physical oceanographers have been analyzing each layer of the ocean and they can now, for example, tell the distinguishing characteristics of Pacific bottom water from Atlantic bottom water.

Physical oceanographers also study circulation patterns of the oceans. One such study involving the Arctic Ocean was undertaken to confirm that there are two separate circulation systems in that ocean—two circular movements of water. After drilling holes in the ice in many locations, measurements of the temperature and density distribution of Arctic Ocean waters were taken. On the basis of this information, it was concluded that there was an undersea mountain ridge dividing the water and that this ridge affected the circulation of the water underneath, causing two different clockwise movements of water.

Other forces affecting the movement of water in the ocean are the tides created by the gravitational interaction of the sun, earth, and moon. Anyone who has lived by the ocean or visited it for any length of time is aware that the height of the tide varies with the moon's monthly cycle. Twice each month— at new moon and full moon—the sun, moon, and earth are aligned so that the pulls of the sun and the moon cause the highest tide, called spring tide. During the first and third quarters of the moon, we have a tide of minimum range called neap tide. As the moon moves around the earth, its gravitational pull sets up an oscillating motion in all the oceans. As the earth rotates, varying daily tides are created as well, depending on the ocean depths, the shape of the coastlines around them, and the sea floor beneath them. In some parts of the world there may be only one high and one low tide per day. This is called a diurnal (daily) tide. In other parts of the world—Europe, for example—there are usually two high tides and two low tides per day. These are called semidiurnal (semidaily) tides.

Localized conditions also cause differences in tides. For example, some elongated bays, such as the Bay of Fundy, which is between Nova Scotia and New Brunswick in Canada and is open to the sea, are subject to the combined effect of both its own natural oscillation and the periodic rush of Atlantic Ocean water into its space. The tides in the Bay of Fundy are among the highest in the world, the range from low to high water there being fifty-three feet.

Oceans have great, sometimes destructive energy. We are certainly aware of the surface waves that rock our boats and smash up against the shore. The force of wave energy also erodes coastal land. In 1870, for example, a 208-foot brick lighthouse—the highest in the world at that time—was built in Cape Hatteras off the coast of North Carolina to warn ships away from the dangerous Diamond Shoals. Originally, the lighthouse stood about 2000 feet inland. However, over the years, with the steady beat of waves against the shore, the beach eroded, and it is feared that the lighthouse, which now stands only 125 feet from the water at high tide, may be toppled into the sea by future storms.

One technique being used to halt erosion near the lighthouse is the use of an artificial seaweed called Seascape. Rows of synthetic fronds are "planted" offshore parallel to the beach. The fronds slow the ocean's current, causing the sand carried by the current to drop to the ocean bottom between the fronds and the lighthouse.

One of the most fearful combinations of wave energy is the tsunami. When there is movement along a fault in the earth's crust, an undersea earthquake occurs which sometimes transmits a powerful energy to the ocean's surface. This shock-wave energy may be dissipated as it travels through thousands of miles of water. But if it meets a land mass, the wave energy is compressed into a smaller space which in turn causes water to shoot upward. The resulting wave may be fifty to one hundred feet high when it hits a shore. Nothing can be done to stop the tsunami, but at least some preparation for its impact can be taken. An international detection and warning system has been established to pinpoint the sources of undersea earthquakes. Ocean-monitoring systems are now able to detect the length, speed, and direction in which potential tsunami waves are moving so that coastal areas in their paths can be warned.

Physical oceanographers and geologists have also discovered that there are equally strong currents beneath the sea. By measuring water temperature and the salt and oxygen contents of muddy bottom water in different parts of the ocean and comparing that against nearby areas, they have discovered that turbidity currents bring water down from upper layers in the ocean. These currents are made up of soft sediments that accumulate on underwater slopes. When they're disturbed by an earthquake, a flood, or simply build up enough density, they slide down the slopes, carrying water with them. We first learned of the power of these underwater currents in 1929, when some of the first transcontinental submarine telegraph cables were snapped into pieces by the pressure of a fifty-mile-an-hour downward avalanche of underwater sediment. Scientists have also discovered that there are currents that carry sediment great distances across the sea floor.

Much of the ocean is still a mystery and scientists have been trying to uncover its secrets for hundreds of years. As is true with any scientific breakthroughs, answers usually come after long, painstaking collections of data to test a hypothesis. Until fairly recently most measurements of currents, surface winds, and temperatures have been taken from the decks of ships. We have already mentioned Benjamin Franklin's charting of the movements of the Gulf Stream. Another pioneer in gathering systematic information on the winds and currents of the world's oceans was Matthew Fontaine Maury, superintendent of the U.S. Navy's Depot of Charts and Instruments. He was able to gather information by encouraging ships' navigators from all over the world to share their oceanic data with him, and by 1851 about 1000 ships were participating in the study. His published charts of winds and currents reduced sailing time from New York to San Francisco, for example, from 180 days to 133 days. Maury's book, *The Physical Geography of the Sea*, published in 1855, was an invaluable guide to sailing ships of the day, and he was also the first to indicate the presence of the "Telegraph Plateau" between Ireland and Newfoundland as ideal for the laying of the first transatlantic telegraph cable.

Today useful information is still gathered from ships. Merchant ships called "ships of opportunity" cooperate with research facilities to provide oceanographic data on temperature of the water, both at the surface and at varying depths down to about 1500 feet below the surface.

Engineers and mathematicians are also involved in helping physical oceanographers find out more about the sea. Learning the mechanics of waves—for instance, how waves transmit energy and under what circumstances they do so—is one way they are involved in today's ocean research. They also investigate ocean pressure and temperature and the velocities of wind, current, and water. If a

Waterspouts, like the one seen here off Grand Bahama Island, are whirling columns of wind and water that extend from the ocean to a cloud. They range from 10 to 5,000 feet high and interior winds can exceed 200 miles per hour.

physical oceanographer formulates a theory on how the energy in the winds over the ocean is transmitted to the actual waves that crash on our beaches, engineers are often called upon to construct laboratory models to simulate ocean conditions. The mathematical calculations developed there can then be tested in the ocean itself. How wind and wave interact, of course, affects the design of ships, the protection of coastlines, and the flow of ocean currents. Similarly, a marine biologist or a chemist might know what he or she wants to investigate but usually needs an engineer to construct the testing equipment. It must be noncorrosive in saltwater; it can't leak; it may have to be a device that releases ballast until it reaches a certain depth in the water, where it then floats; it may have electrical connections. It is so expensive to take a research ship out to an ocean site that it is vitally important that all the mechanical or electrical investigative devices work efficiently.

Deep-sea pressure is one of the most hostile forces of the sea to human beings. While sea-level pressure on the human body is 14.7 pounds per square inch (a measurement known as one atmosphere), the pressure increases by one atmosphere for every thirty-three feet below the surface. This means that a diver would experience a pressure equivalent to 485 pounds per square inch of his or her body when 1000 feet below the surface.

Scientists have long been interested in the effects of deep-sea pressure on the human body because more and more research about marine life as well as offshore oil drilling takes place in depths of over 1000 feet. The shallower waters were investigated first; now we want to know more about the deeper ones. Researchers have made great strides in equipping divers for these conditions. Because it is the air space between the fluid and solid parts of the body that needs to be prepared to withstand compression, divers breathe a mixture that is kept at the same pressure as the water surrounding them. Since oxygen becomes deadly when compressed, a mixture of gases is used. High-pressure nervous syndrome—tremors, vomiting, fatigue, and lapses of consciousness—is experienced by divers at depths greater than 1000 feet. This can be counteracted by nitrogen gas. Nitrogen, however, has a narcotic effect that can range from a dullness of the senses to stupor, coma, or convulsions, so researchers have been experimenting with certain ratios of nitrogen, helium, oxygen, and compression rates in simulated dives to help us learn more about how we can work efficiently at greater depths. A simulated dive of 2250 feet has been achieved, but it required a decompression period of thirty-one days to bring the divers back to sea-level pressure. During compression, the mixture of gases given to the diver is absorbed into the blood and tissues. If the diver returns too quickly to the surface, the gases form bubbles in the blood and joints, which cause the pain known as the "bends," so the mixture of gases and the rate of pressure at which they are given the diver during decompression are very important.

Another answer to deeper diving is the Jim Suit (named after Jim Jarret, the chief diver who worked with inventor Joseph Peress on salvaging the wreck of the *Lusitania* in the 1930s). The Jim Suit allows a diver to work at sea-level pressure in depths of over 1000 feet, since its metal shell effectively withstands the deeper seawater pressure. Although used primarily for work on offshore oil drilling, it also has value for research about marine life.

For dives to the deepest ocean floor, however, special submarine vehicles have been designed. One of the first attempts at deep-sea diving, recorded in historical paintings and engravings, was that by Alexander the Great, who lived in the fourth century B.C. He is said to have been lowered to the sea floor in a diving bell. (You can see how the diving bell worked by taking a glass and turning it upside down in a pan of water. Although a little water is forced into the glass, the balance of the space is a supply of air.) Since the amount of air inside a bell is gradually used up by breathing, later versions included pipes and hoses to supply air. Today our technology has become so sophisticated that we have nuclear-powered submarines that can travel for months without refueling or resurfacing.

Some of our information about the oceans comes not from the sea but from the sky. Satellites are used to create television images of broad areas of the Pacific, for example, and to relay reports by radio instruments from buoys set out across that ocean. The University of Miami's Rosenstiel School of Marine and Atmospheric Science and the Scripps Institution of Oceanography were among the first to establish a satellite station at an oceanographic research center to provide immediate reports on marine conditions. By using satellites, scientists can observe remote locations where ships can't go and can also see larger areas at one time. And they can have all the information almost instantly.

Early satellite pictures were like the weather maps in your daily newspaper. Then instruments were developed to photograph the amount of infrared radiation (from which the temperature of water could be deduced) and the varying color of ocean water (from which the amount of chlorophyll and marine life can be determined). Since what the satellite cameras could see was affected by the amount of clouds between the satellite and the earth, microwave radiometers, which measure electromagnetic radiation, were added; these could penetrate the clouds and give sharper images.

Remote sensing—that is, making observations electronically—is also accomplished by installing measuring instruments and radio equipment on buoys in the ocean; these transmit information on winds, current movements, temperatures, and other ocean data to satellites, which then retransmit the data to the oceanographic receiving station.

Because the space shuttle *Columbia* on its second mission in November 1981 flew much lower than most satellites, the radar pictures it brought back provided images that were much more detailed. One series—showing unexpected large surface waves in the Mediterranean—is now being studied by oceanographers.

One great disappointment for oceanographers was the loss of *SEASAT*, the first American satellite specifically designed for studying the oceans. It was launched on June 28, 1978, but had a working life of only three months. In October 1978, it failed as a result of an electrical problem. *SEASAT* carried five monitoring instruments. Only one of these, the microwave radiometer, is now carried on another existing satellite, *NIMBUS-7*. Whether government funding will be made available for another satellite to study the oceans remains to be seen.

Remote sensing of the oceans by satellite is useful not only to meteorologists, oceanographers, and atmospheric scientists, but also the public. Shippers who must cross the polar regions now have more accurate information on the location and movent of icebergs, public and private developers can obtain information on erosion and sediment movement around beaches, we can track oil spills, and we can locate likely fishing grounds by looking at ocean color and calculating the amount of chlorophyll there.

Satellites can relay information to us about the content and movement of the water in the oceans of the world. They can also tell us something about the topography of the ocean floor in shallower areas and about the gravity fields of the earth's crust. But they can't tell us yet about the mineral content of the crust. That we must investigate in other ways.

2

THE OCEAN FLOOR

When Mt. St. Helens erupted in Washington we saw firsthand the awesome power of a volcano on land. That same pent-up energy is found beneath the sea. When an underwater volcano erupts as it lies just under the surface, the lava spews out and settles back on top of the volcano to form an island in the sea. For instance, that is how the island of Surtsey was formed off the coast of Iceland in 1963 when an underwater volcano erupted. Land dwellers tend to think of the ocean as a big bowl of water, but the bottom of the sea is as full of mountains and canyons and valleys as the surface of the earth is. In fact, the longest mountain range in the world, the Mid-Ocean Ridge, is under water. It winds its way in an S-shape across the Atlantic Ocean floor and then continues on to the Indian and Pacific oceans. And the highest mountain in the world is not Everest, but rather Mauna Kea—actually a dormant volcano on the island of Hawaii. It is 33,476 feet from its base at the bottom of the ocean to its peak on land. (You could put Mt. Everest down in the deepest part of the ocean and there would still be one mile of water between its peak and the ocean's surface.)

The crust of the earth under land is granitic rock over a layer of basaltic rock; the crust at the bottom of the sea, on the other hand, is basaltic rock covered mostly by sediment. With the help of depth-sounding equipment developed after World Wars I and II we have finally been able to map the ocean floor.

Most of the research to date has involved the coastal lands and waters. According to geologists, the seabed along our coasts has three sections: that nearest the shore is called the continental shelf; next, a continental slope levels off temporarily to a continental rise; and, finally, the rise ends at the abyssal (deep-sea) plain, the flat part of the ocean bottom.

If all the water were to be drained from the oceans, you'd notice that some coastlines (like the one in New England) have shelves extending out several hundred miles from the shore, while others (like the west coast of South America) drop off into deep water very soon.

The ocean bottom nearest to the shore is of great concern to the nations that depend upon natural resources such as seaweed, fish, or oil for their economic well-being. About 50 percent of all fish we harvest for food are found in coastal areas, since the plants and animals on which they feed thrive at water depths the sun's rays can penetrate. Far Eastern countries depend on seaweed growing near coastlines for more than 20 percent of their daily diet. And 37 percent of the proved oil and gas resources that have been located in the ocean so far are on the continental shelf.

Scientists are concerned about the erosion of the marshes and wetlands that lie at the edges of coastal shores. Some rivers, like the Mississippi, build up barrier islands from river sediment at their deltas; these barriers protect the marshes behind them. But if the islands are eroded away—either by the force of waves or by changing currents in the ocean—saltwater can then flow into the marshes and destroy the freshwater life that is found there. The canals dug in marshes for oil and gas exploration are another cause of con-

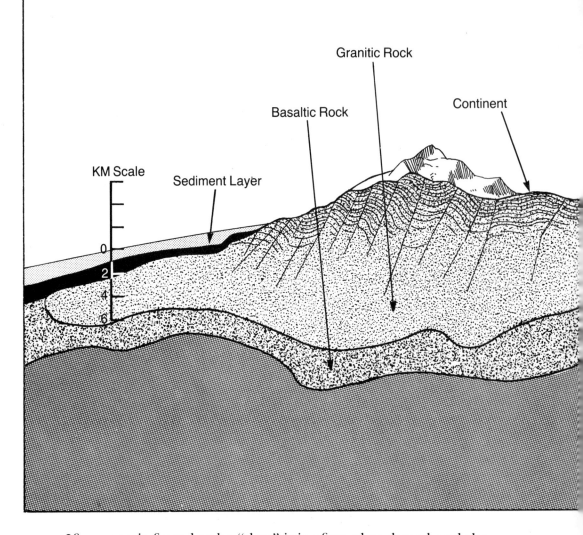

KM Scale

Sediment Layer

Basaltic Rock

Granitic Rock

Continent

0
2
4
6

cern. If an area is found to be "dry," it is often abandoned and the canals left unfilled. It is estimated that over 50 percent of coastal land in some areas of Louisiana, for example, is lost because of this. If the canals were to be filled in, say some researchers, the eroding away of the land could be prevented and the marshes kept safe for freshwater plants and organisms.

Geologists have always been interested in the structure of the earth's crust, and their explorations with deep-sea drilling are gradually revealing the age of the ocean crust and the location that

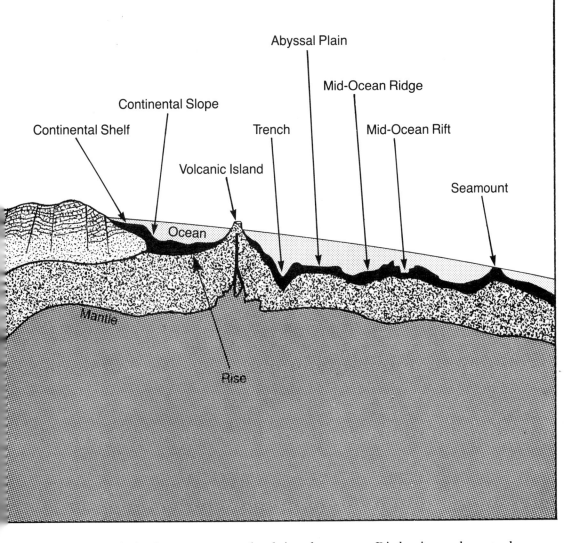

Continental Shelf
Continental Slope
Volcanic Island
Trench
Abyssal Plain
Mid-Ocean Ridge
Mid-Ocean Rift
Seamount
Ocean
Mantle
Rise

land and sea masses had in the past. Biologists who study pre-historic plants and animals in order to place them in the evolution-ary scale are also involved in these studies. So are chemists and physicists, since the rocks of our planet are composed of mineral elements, and the earth has magnetic and electrical properties as well. The earth's crust is thinner under the ocean (about three miles thick) than it is on land (about thirty miles), and much scien-tific research on the crust takes place underwater.

Geologists credit Leonardo da Vinci with being one of the first to recognize that fossils of marine animals found high up in the Apennines, a mountain chain in Italy, were similar to the species of marine animals that lived in the Mediterranean. He speculated that the Mediterranean and the land had not always been in the same relationship to each other as they were when he saw them.

Today's scientists would agree with da Vinci. The earth's crust is not fixed—it is always subject to change. The theory of plate tectonics says that the earth is made up of huge movable plates that are about fifty miles thick; these separate from each other at the midocean ridges and come together at deep-sea trenches. When these plates collide, they may push up huge mountain ranges, such as the Himalayas, from the crust. When the plates break apart, they may fragment into new continents and form new oceans through the creation of new crust. Such movements may account for earthquakes such as those that occur along the San Andreas Fault in California. In fact, most of what we know about the inside of the earth comes from the study of earthquakes and from the fact that seismic, or shock waves, the vibrations caused by these earthquakes, travel at different speeds through different densities of rock and bend at certain depths in the earth where the rock type changes. Seismologists who study earthquakes and other phenomena of the earth have divided the inside of our planet into three major sections: an outer crust, which is from three to thirty miles thick; a mantle, 1800 miles of gradually denser rock; and a 2100-mile-thick, even denser core.

Geologists have been able to use this information in their study of the earth's crust at ocean bottom. In the "youngest" part of the ocean, where the ocean floor has spread apart in the rift valley "crack" of the Mid-Ocean Ridge, lava that bubbled up from the earth's interior and solidified to become basalt can be observed and photographed by cameras on submarine research-vessels. But in older parts of the ocean, where millions of years of sediment have piled up on top of the basaltic crust, the only way to get to the earth's crust is by deep-sea drilling.

Scientists have been seeking information about the earth's crust for years, although deep-sea drilling is a twentieth-century phenomenon. The first ship to be devoted exclusively to oceanographic exploration was the H.M.S. *Challenger*, a British vessel that in 1872 made a three-and-a-half-year voyage through the Atlantic, Pacific, and Indian oceans. It took depth soundings and collected samples of marine life, plants, and minerals from different levels of the ocean and the seabed, providing a wealth of data on the subsurface. Another early investigation of the bottom depths was conducted from 1838 to 1842 by the U.S. Exploring Expedition, led by Naval Lieutenant Charles Wilkes, who was one of the first to map the Antarctic coast and deep sea. These early explorers had to take soundings by hand—a difficult process. A lead-weighted line was let down until it touched bottom. After the depth was noted, the line was retrieved, the ship moved about ten miles, and another sounding was taken. Depending on the depth reached by the lead, the time necessary to complete a single sounding could range from one to several hours. This laborious process was replaced only in 1920 with the development of echo-sounding equipment and, eventually, with other technology evolved during World War II.

Now, more than 100 years after the voyages of the *Challenger*, its American namesake, the D/V (for "Drilling Vessel") *Glomar Challenger*, a large ship with a drilling derrick on its deck 194 feet above the waterline, is attempting to unlock the secrets of the earth's crust and of the ocean basins. The Deep Sea Drilling Project, which is managed by the Scripps Institution of Oceanography under a contract with the National Science Foundation, has been exploring the sea floor this way since 1968. In 1975, scientists from more than twenty nations participated in the voyages of this unique vessel. Members of the Joint Oceanographic Institutions for Deep

The most significant discovery of the Wilkes Exploring Expedition was the Antarctic Continent, previously thought to be only ice.

Earth Sampling (JOIDES) provided scientific planning for its expeditions.

Scientists on the *Glomar Challenger* have learned many exciting things. They have discovered, for example, that the oldest dated rocks recovered from the sea floor are about 160 million years old. Since the oldest rocks found on land are about four billion years old, scientists have concluded that the oceanic crust is much "younger" than the surrounding land. We are able to tell how old a rock is by examining its radioactive elements. The age of these elements can be measured by the amount of time it takes for them to decay. Uranium, for instance, has a very slow decaying process—one that requires billions of years—so that when we measure the amount of radioactivity still remaining in a rock we know how old it is.

Measuring the depth of water was a laborious hand process before modern depth-sound technology. A heavy weight attached to a line was payed out by men standing on the projecting ledges of the chain-wales as the captain held the ship steady in the wind.

33

The size of this test miner can be seen by comparison with the worker in the lower left corner. Note, too, that the test miner is shown inside the vast center well of the *Glomar Explorer*.

Drilling samples from the submerged midocean ridges and other samples from the deep-sea trenches were also taken by *Glomar Challenger* scientists. Measurements of the radioactive elements in the samples showed varying ages of the sea bottom and confirmed the geophysical theories that the sea floor has been spreading at the rate of from 0.4 to 5 inches (1 to 13 centimeters) per year, and that this can explain the drifting apart of the continents. Other samples have shown that some underwater seamounts (mountains beneath the sea) have deep-sea sediments overlaying land-type sediments. To scientists this indicates that vertical motions of the earth's crust that thrust up mountains can also have caused other land forms to sink slowly beneath the sea.

Small animals and plants that the scientists recovered from the Mediterranean indicate that that sea had completely dried up about twelve million years ago. Its opening to the ocean at the Strait

34

of Gibraltar had temporarily closed, and evaporation of its waters exceeded the amount of water it could receive as rain or from river input. About seven million years later, however, it filled up again and has been a two-mile-deep sea ever since.

Our need to know more about earthquakes and how fast their shock waves travel through the earth prompted a research expedition made by a number of other ships into the mouth of the Gulf of California, an area that produces many quakes. By lowering seventy submersible seismometers (instruments that measure shock waves) and then detonating specific amounts of explosives, scientists from the United States, Europe, and Mexico were able to chart more accurately the shock-wave velocities passing through the undersea areas.

The results of voyages the *Glomar Challenger* made in November and December of 1980 have led some scientists to speculate that the Atlantic appeared possibly 155 million years ago, about twenty to thirty million years later than was previously believed. This estimate was reached by learning the age of the microscopic fossil remains of marine organisms imbedded in the mud samples brought up from the ocean floor in the hollow pipe "cores" that had been drilled into the undersea earth's crust.

One of the important undertakings of the *Glomar Challenger* has been the building up of a "library" of sediment samples from various parts of the seabed. These help scientists to catalog the fossils buried there and to trace the evolution of the many organisms that have lived in the oceans. The library of drilling cores containing sediment samples brought up from the seabeds of the Pacific and Indian oceans are kept at the Scripps Institution of Oceanography in La Jolla, California; and samples from the Atlantic, Antarctic, and the Mediterranean are stored at the Lamont-Doherty Geological Observatory of Columbia University, in Palisades, New York.

While the majority of the work done by the *Glomar Challenger* involves scientific research, the tools developed for its work have been valuable to commercial operations as well. In the early days of the drilling, for example, whenever the drill bit boring the hole wore out (the sea bottom is not always soft sediment), the entire length of drill pipe had to be recovered and the hole abandoned. Reinserting a new drill bit into the original hole would have been like trying to locate a tiny ten-inch hole in the dark at the bottom of a 15,000-foot pool of water while in a ship being tossed about by wind and waves. Project engineers solved this problem by creating a reentry cone: a steel funnel, sixteen feet in diameter, located over the drill hole and equipped with sonar (sound navigation and ranging) reflectors to reflect sound impulses sent to it. When a bit wears out, the drill pipe can be brought back to the surface and a new bit attached. This new bit can then be lowered with a sonar device, which can send out signals to be echoed back from the reflector on the reentry cone over the drill hole, permitting the drill string and bit to be positioned directly over it for reentering the drill hole. Instruments can also be inserted into the drill hole the same way and left for long-term recording.

Another device that has been adopted by drilling ships around the world is computer-controlled dynamic positioning. The ship is equipped with engines at its bow and stern to move it sideways as needed—to keep it exactly over the bore hole in midocean. Still another refinement has been the heave-compensator system, which keeps the drill string separate from the up-and-down (heave) motion of the ship as the ship is affected by wind and wave. This provides greater control and reduces the possibility of loss and breakage of the drill string.

Scientists are not the only persons interested in the seabed. Since the continental shelves directly adjacent to most coastlines contain the majority of the fish we eat, the ownership of these

36

shelves is an important economic consideration. And the developing technology for offshore oil drilling adds another group concerned with the ownership of the continental shelves.

How far from its coastline does a nation have the right to claim exclusive use? The historical three-mile limit was established because that was how far a cannonball could be shot from shore in order to protect a nation's rights to its coastal waters. In recent years, however, individual countries have begun making claims for much longer distances so they could reserve for themselves the natural resources that might be found there.

In a 1975 session of the United Nations Law of the Sea Treaty Conference, participating countries agreed that the continental shelf of a coastal nation extended to 200 nautical miles (a nautical mile is 6076 feet) from its coastline. Coastal nations were given the exclusive right to authorize and regulate drilling on the shelf and to construct artificial islands or other installations in this region. They were also required to ensure compliance with international standards to protect the marine environment from pollution. In cases where adjacent nations were claiming the same waters, rules were established for sharing on an equitable basis or for negotiating a settlement. Subsequent meetings of the Law of the Sea Treaty Conference refined these rules more specifically in an attempt to obtain agreement on each coastal nation's rights to control passage on the sea near its shores (up to twelve miles) and its exclusive rights to exploitation of an economic zone (up to 200 miles).

Individual countries have also established rules for the use of the natural resources found on their continental shelves. In the United States, for example, President Harry Truman established a legal precedent in 1945, by ruling that an individual state couldn't claim the right to the oil deposits on the land off its shore—only the federal government could. But that also meant that the United States was establishing a claim for itself against the attempts of other nations to do so. As might be expected, coastal states challenged this doctrine in the courts and attempted to change the ruling through Congress. As a result, the Submerged Lands Act of 1953 returned anywhere from three miles to three marine leagues (nine miles) to each coastal state, depending on what the boundary was when the state joined the Union. On the other hand, in that same year, the Outer Continental Shelf Lands Act reaffirmed that the coastal shelf beyond state boundaries was subject to the control of the federal government.

3

ENERGY FROM THE SEA

The ocean is a huge energy machine. Working with the sun, it warms or cools our atmosphere. The strength of its waves and currents help supply our electricity. Companies drill its seabed for oil and develop sophisticated technology to scoop mineral-rich nodules off its deep floor. Scientists are trying to discover how to best utilize the energy these vast ocean waters contain.

The transfer of heat energy from the ocean has a great effect on the world atmosphere: the heat causes water evaporation, forming freshwater clouds that release rain or snow; and heat radiated from the ocean is also sent up into air above the water. Both the heated air and the heated ocean water are carried to other parts of the earth by wind and current. Scientists are trying to understand what it is that causes one winter to have bone-chilling blizzards and the next to be warmer than usual. They want to find out which aspects of climate are predictable. The study of oceans and their effect on the atmosphere is one aspect of this search.

We know, for example, that hot air rising from the equator

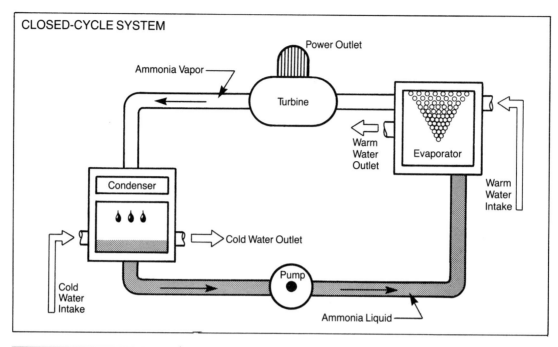

CLOSED-CYCLE SYSTEM

Power Outlet

Ammonia Vapor

Turbine

Warm Water Outlet

Evaporator

Warm Water Intake

Condenser

Cold Water Outlet

Cold Water Intake

Pump

Ammonia Liquid

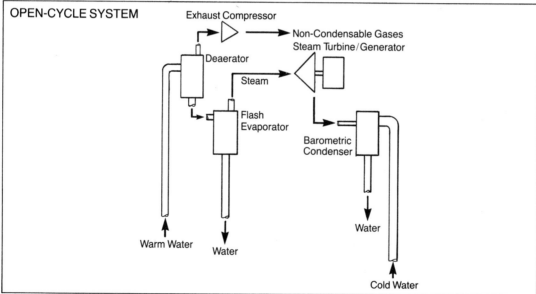

OPEN-CYCLE SYSTEM

Exhaust Compressor

Non-Condensable Gases
Steam Turbine/Generator

Deaerator

Steam

Flash Evaporator

Barometric Condenser

Warm Water

Water

Water

Cold Water

Two experimental proposals for converting ocean thermal energy into electrical power are the "open loop" and "closed loop" systems. The open loop system evaporates seawater to create steam to turn a turbine; the closed loop system uses sea water to heat ammonia whose expanding gases drive a turbine.

expands and creates a low-pressure area. At the poles, sinking cool air creates a high-pressure area, and the polar air moves from high-pressure to low-pressure area toward the equator. But since the earth rotates, the air doesn't flow in a straight line. Rather, because of the Coriolis effect (named after Gaspard Gustave de Coriolis, a French mathematician, who first described this phenomenon of air flow in 1835), the air turns toward the right in the northern hemisphere and to the left in the southern hemisphere. Since sun, wind, currents, water temperature, and earth rotation are all interacting simultaneously, scientists have yet to unravel completely the causes and effects of the world's atmosphere.

There is research in the tropics, however, that holds the promise of a solar energy source from the oceans that the world can take advantage of. For three months in 1979, the world's first ocean thermal energy conversion (OTEC) plant was built and operated in Hawaii to demonstrate that the technology could generate electric power. It was a "closed-loop" system in which warm surface ocean water heated by the sun was used to vaporize liquid ammonia gas. As the gas expanded, it drove a turbine, which produced electricity. Cold water (about 40° F) from 2500 feet below the surface of the ocean was pumped up and used to condense the ammonia back to a liquid and the process repeated. OTEC has several important advantages. First, the ocean is free and is available twenty-four hours a day, whereas other solar energy devices are affected by the difference in temperature between night and day or by cloudy weather. Second, because OTEC depends on the difference in temperature between warm surface water and the colder water below—the greater the difference in temperature, the greater the efficiency—the warm surface water of the tropics (about 80° F) makes locations like Hawaii or the Caribbean ideal for the operation. A third advantage is that the process does not pollute the environment, although environmentalists are concerned that the

An ocean thermal energy conversion power plant of the future, designed to generate enough power for a population of 200,000 people. The subsurface plant contains crew quarters and maintenance facilities.

cold water discharged near the ocean's surface could cool the surrounding local waters and thereby affect marine life. On the other hand, future OTEC plants may be anchored offshore in deeper waters, where there is less marine life to be sucked into its pipes or foul the heat-exchange surfaces.

The power of a waterfall can drive electricity-generating equipment. But there is another, not quite as dramatic, source of energy in those parts of the world where tidal waves regularly exist. If a naturally high tide flows into an estuary close enough to a city or other project needing electricity, a dam can be built to store a large reservoir of power-producing water there. The Rance tidal-power station at St.-Malo, France, completed in 1967, is such a dam. The operating principle is the same as the one used for the small tidal mills that were built along many coastlines in the past. The owners of these mills took advantage of the tide to build dikes that created storage basins in coves. Gates were used to allow the basin to fill up at flood tide. At ebb tide, when the water flowed out, the paddles on a partially submerged wheel were turned by the force of the water, and the wheel was used to drive a grinding mill. These mills, which produced power only during the twice-daily tidal cycles, were "single-acting": they could operate only when the water was flowing out. The Rance tidal-power station, however, is constructed so that the turbines can be used in both water-flow directions: power can be produced both during the filling and the emptying of the basin. Also, if extra seawater is pumped into the basin at the end of the filling cycle, there is an increase in power production when the water flows back out.

Still another natural phenomenon of the ocean—circulating-current systems—is a possible source of energy. In 1835 de Coriolis published a paper that analyzed not only the deflection of wind flow due to the earth's rotation, as mentioned earlier in this chapter, but also showed that the waters in the ocean are similarly affected. According to the Coriolis effect, a moving object tends to curve to the right in the northern hemisphere and to the left in the southern hemisphere. This effect intensifies the circulating ocean current in the western portion of the North Atlantic—the Gulf Stream—so that the Florida Current, which is part of it, contains fifty times more energy than all the rivers of the world combined. Scientists believe that the energy of such ocean currents could be used to drive large marine turbines moored below the surface. Engineers are working on experimental designs that would place an array of large ocean turbines in the Florida Current. Each turbine would be about 560 feet in diameter and the initial system would produce 10,000 megawatts of electricity—the energy equivalent of about 130 million barrels of oil per year onshore.

Gas harvested from the sea gives us another potential energy source. For example, seaweed such as kelp, the species that grows off the California coast, can be processed into methane gas. Kelp grows at a fantastic rate—sometimes as much as two feet per day—and efforts are being made to grow kelp two feet every day. If this can be done, ten acres of kelp could be harvested and turned into as much as six million cubic feet of gas a year.

Another proposed experiment is to move the rich deposits of natural gas found in Prudhoe Bay, Alaska, by using a fleet of huge 950,000-ton submarine supertankers. Each submarine would be designed to carry thirty-seven million gallons of liquefied natural gas chilled to minus 260° F. The submarine would move the gas 3200 miles, from beneath the arctic ice cap to ports on the east coast of Canada and to Europe.

A major source of energy today is oil. Because the world depends so heavily on oil as its primary energy source, there is great concern that unless we continue to discover new deposits, demand will increase beyond our known supplies by about the year 2000. Since about 37 percent of presently known oil reserves are off-

An oil drilling rig must be solidly positioned to withstand the buffeting of wind and waves and to provide a safe, temporary home for its crews.

shore, and some companies think there is a better chance of finding large fields there than on land, efforts are being made to unlock these reservoirs of energy.

How did the oil get there? Organic matter from plants and animals sank to the seabed and was covered by sediment. Over millions of years, heat and pressure converted this organic matter into liquid or gaseous hydrocarbons. However, the existence of the hydrocarbons alone will not create oil or gas fields. A number of conditions must occur at the right place and at the right time. Oil must migrate into a geologic "trap" over a span of time long enough to allow the petroleum to accumulate. This trap is a layer of porous (reservoir) rock called the sedimentary basin.

Oil companies know from experience that sedimentary basins on the continental shelves are likely prospects for deposits of oil and gas. These shelves also have shallower water, which makes it easier to set up drilling rigs. But companies also use modern technology to search for other deposits in the open sea. One such tool is the seismic prospecting ship, whose purpose is to record detailed information about the rocks underneath the crust of the sea bottom over which it is traveling. Technicians aboard the ship feed out from its stern a long cable containing hydrophones—sound wave detectors. An energy source is released (such as explosives or bursts of compressed air) from another trailing device. The released energy waves penetrate the rocks below and are then reflected back to the detectors in the tube. The findings are recorded on magnetic tape, fed into a computer, and analyzed. Geologists can combine this information with other knowledge about the rocks by using tools such as magnetometers, which measure the magnetic intensities of different rock types to reveal their characteristics. Since most oil is found in rocks that are at least two million years old, geologist-prospectors can concentrate on areas known through scientific exploratory drilling to contain such formations.

The types of oil drilling rigs used today are designed to cope with the weather conditions, wave heights during sea storms, and the need for a rig to be taken down and moved to another site if the well does not prove productive. Three main types of drilling rigs have emerged. In water up to about 300 feet, the jackup rig is used most often. It is towed to the site, where its legs are lowered to the seabed and the platform is jacked up 100 feet or to a safe height above sea level. Although it then provides a fixed drilling platform and its initial cost is less than for other types, it has the disadvantage of being difficult to tow, with its 400-foot towers on board, to the drilling site, which may be a long distance from its construction location. It is also subject to accidents during the jacking-up procedure if the weather is bad, creating unexpectedly poor sea conditions.

The second type of rig is the semisubmersible, which was developed as the search for oil pushed farther into deeper water. It can function at depths of up to 2500 feet. Towed or self-propelled to the site, it is lowered to working position by flooding pontoonlike ballast chambers with seawater to stabilize it against winds and waves. The superstructure remains at a safe height above the sea. Its mooring lines, which may extend a mile or more, are held in place by anchors weighing up to twenty tons.

The third type is the drill ship, which can operate in 6000 or more feet of water. The ship has a walled opening through its hull for drilling, and it maintains its position over the drill site either by mooring anchors or by motor-driven propeller thrusters at the bow and stern—the procedure developed by the *Glomar Challenger*. Drill ships can transport large supplies of drilling equipment, but they cannot operate in sea conditions that produce excessive platform motion.

Movies of land-oil discoveries have familiarized us with the picture of roughnecks lowering a drill bit into a turntable in a rig floor. That same procedure is used by hard-hatted oil rig workers at sea today. But what happens at the other end of the drill? Usually the first hole drilled is to contain a thirty-inch diameter steel conductor casing, which is cemented into place. After this first string of casing is set in the hole, which may be 200 feet deep, and cemented, a blowout preventor (BOP) is installed at the wellhead at the top of this casing. The BOP contains valves that can close off the space between the drill pipe and the casing, or open hole, in a matter of seconds if unexpected changes in pressures are detected. After the BOP is in place, drilling continues with smaller bits in order to install more cemented steel casing, until the drill reaches the area where geologists have decided that oil is likely to be found. One of the technicians on the rig is the "mud engineer," who supervises the fluids used in the drill pipe to cool and lubricate the drill bit and to bring back cuttings to the surface. The drilling process is constantly monitored, and sensing devices detect when fluid is being lost to the drilled formation or when gas or saltwater is seeping into the hole made by the drill bit. Either condition may indicate a change in well pressure.

Once oil is discovered in one location, wells are drilled nearby to determine how large the field is and whether it is economical to develop it. If the findings are positive, the next step is the construction of a production platform facility containing all the equipment necessary to keep oil flowing from the discovered well to storage facilities and to house the crew while the oil is being produced. How the platform will be constructed depends on several factors. Is the water shallow and the sea bottom soft, as in the Gulf of Mexico? Are there boulders on the floor, as in the North Sea, where it would be difficult to drive piles and a concrete gravity structure would be better? (These huge concrete columns rest on the bottom of the ocean, and at the base of their concrete legs are cells with storage for up to one million barrels of oil—making the structure's gross weight ten times that of steel.) Would a floating platform be preferable? Is the area susceptible to earthquakes or hurricanes? Is the sea covered by abrasive ice much of the time? There may be a time lag of up to five years from the time when the exploratory well is dug and the day when the the first barrel of crude oil is delivered. How will the oil be brought to shore? Decisions also have to be made about storage facilities and loading or transmission systems.

Until remote technology was developed, underwater construction required human beings to go down to direct, inspect, or maintain it. Special equipment was needed to help the diver's body cope with the underwater pressure and perform strenuous work at the same time. As mentioned in Chapter 1, the deeper a diver goes into the water, the greater is the pressure of the water on the body and on the air in the lungs. To combat this, the diver breathes a mixture of gases that has the same pressure as is found in the depth of the water in which he or she will work.

But today, the most modern undersea production facilities are completely remote-controlled. Special techniques are used to install the wellhead and to drill the well from the drilling vessel. The wells are serviced and maintained by equipment right in the well itself or by unmanned, remote-controlled vehicles.

One unusual indirect energy source, about whose existence we have known for more than 100 years, is the mineral-rich nodules on the sea floor. They were first brought up from the sea floor by the *Challenger* in the 1870s and were for the most part considered curiosities to be seen in the British Museum until recent studies of the ocean turned scientists' attention to them. These lumps, which look a bit like baked potatoes, contain manganese, copper, nickel, cobalt, and molybdenum. Industrial nations, which need nickel and manganese for steel production and cobalt to use for the superalloys from which jet engines are made, are developing the technology to retrieve these nodules. Since steel is a major material used in the construction of oil- and gas-drilling rigs, and copper is a primary material for electric transmission cables, these minerals are extremely important to energy industries.

Mineral-rich manganese nodules such as these are of prime importance to industrial nations.

Although we don't know exactly how the nodules are formed, they usually accumulate around a bit of organic material from the ocean floor—a shark's tooth, for example, or a piece of shell. How fast they grow is also unknown. Some samples have been radioactively dated as growing one millimeter per 1,000,000 years; others have been found growing on manmade objects we know are only twenty or thirty years old. Recoverable amounts of the known land sources of minerals are limited, according to some forecasters, so this could be another continuing mineral "farm" under the sea. However, the high cost of retrieving these nodules (they lie in the deep ocean, 12,000 to 20,000 feet down) as well as controversies over territorial rights have delayed the task of harvesting them.

Scientists are constantly looking for new energy sources from the sea and are certain that there are many such sources yet to be discovered. One of the most powerful ones used in World War II was uranium, the metallic element that fueled the atomic bomb. Uranium also has peaceful uses. It is the element used in nuclear power plants—a compact heat source for the steam to turn turbines that produce electricity for our cities. In terms of energy produced, one pound of uranium is equal to 2000 tons of coal. While it is estimated that the land deposits of the world's available uranium are about two million tons, scientists estimate there are four billion tons in the oceans. A Japanese scientist has developed a filtering process he says could help energy-poor Japan to extract uranium from seawater. The process uses a form of titanous oxide, which triggers uranium to form into a mass. At present the process is still more costly than land mining of uranium, but research is proceeding.

A West German scientist has discovered a species of Black Sea plankton that is capable of absorbing uranium. The plankton were found in sediment from cores drilled into the Black Sea bottom. Uranium which had been dissolved in the Black Sea was picked up by the proteins and sugars in the planktons' bodies, until the concentration of uranium increased 10,000-fold in the plankton. These tiny organisms died and sank to the sea bottom over a period of 5,000 years. Since these uranium-rich plankton sediments occur at depths of 3,500 to 7,000 feet, mining them would be difficult. But could there be a way to isolate and then synthesize the proteins and natural sugars in the bodies of uranium-attracting species of plankton so that the synthetic chemical could be used as a uranium gatherer in seawater? It's a theory for scientists to investigate.

Because future energy needs are expected to increase significantly, it is essential that studies and experiments of this sort continue to explore a variety of energy sources to meet future world demand.

4

MARINE LIFE

In 1977, a Japanese trawler off New Zealand netted the remains of a thirty-foot, 4000-pound sea creature. One marine biologist—from examining photographs—said it resembled the plesiosaurus, an extinct sea reptile that lived 130 million years ago. Another said it may only have been the misinterpretation of a decayed known animal such as a basking shark. In any case, its five-foot neck, six-foot tail, and front and rear fins made it a monstrous sight indeed. Was it the appearance of such creatures that struck fear into the hearts of early sailors setting out on uncharted seas or did their imaginations create even more horrible adversaries? We know that some forms of sea plants can be a hundred feet long. Such plants, as thick as a man's body and undulating on the waves, could have been taken for sea serpents. Whatever sailors saw or imagined, however, pales beside the infinite variety of life in the sea, as we are gradually discovering.

In their quest for solutions to these mysteries, marine biologists today draw upon a long history of speculation concerning

what kinds of living things exist in the ocean and upon the reports of persons who actually examined what is there. Aristotle was one of the first students of marine life. His *Historia Animalium,* written in the fourth century B.C., described 180 different species of Aegean Sea fauna.

The dramatic voyages of the British ship *Beagle* around the world from 1831 to 1836, in which Charles Darwin collected much of his data on the natural history of both land and sea, explored both coasts of South America, Tierra del Fuego, the Galapagos Islands, and Australia. And in 1842, Edward Forbes of Great Britain chose the Aegean to study the distribution of species as they live in different depths of the ocean. Years ago biologists assumed that animal life could not exist at deeper levels because of the intense pressure found there and because of the lack of light. But deep-sea photos, marine animals brought up in traps, and a series of dives by

Sea serpents appear in both Eastern and Western legends. Norwegian sailors, for example, reported that the sea serpent would cast himself in the path of a vessel, rise suddenly and seize one of the frightened crew as prey.

the deep-sea submersible vehicle *Alvin,* developed by the Woods Hole Oceanographic Institution, helped disprove this. Scientists discovered active hot springs on the ocean floor in the Galapagos Rift Zone of the Pacific that changed their thinking about how life can exist without sunlight.

While geologists were studying the springs because the hot water bubbling up from the interior of the earth brings minerals with it and deposits them on the ocean floor, they unexpectedly discovered a unique ecosystem of marine life. (An ecosystem is a life-cycle composed of plants, animals, and decomposers.) Scientists found clams almost a foot long, mussels, crabs, sea anemones, and other organisms in 9000-foot-deep water, where no sunlight penetrates. Scientists formerly believed that photosynthesis—the process by which plants use sunlight energy to make carbohydrates from carbon dioxide and water—was the source of all life in the ocean, but here was life that defied that theory. Instead, bacteria living in the ocean were using a process called chemosynthesis to derive the energy needed to synthesize organic compounds from the hydrogen sulfide contained in the hot springs. In chemosynthesis, chemical reactions (rather than the sun) provide the

The bottom dweller Sea Star's Latin name *Astropecten duplicatus* comes from the Greek word for star and the Latin for rake—referring to the even rows of projections along each arm.

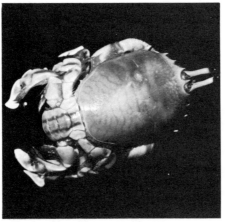

Frog Crabs are often dredged from offshore sandy bottoms. They have flattened major claws on the first legs, which are tucked under the body in this photograph.

The major claws of the female Coral Crab are the same size; the males have one larger than the other—called the fighting claw.

energy to create the organic compounds of life. Such bacteria provide the start of the food chain by being eaten by clams and mussels, which then provide food for other organisms.

One of the scientists studying these deep-sea bacteria, a marine biologist at the Scripps Institution in California, was able to bring up live, shrimplike crustaceans called amphipods from six miles down in the Pacific's Mariana Trench by using pressurized traps. The amphipods were captured at a depth of about 34,500 feet, where pressures are greater than 15,000 pounds per square inch and the temperature is about 2° C.

One outcome of this research and the study of bacterial activity on the decomposing carcasses is the belief that the physical systems that have enabled these bacteria to survive at such great pressures and low temperatures may have applications for industrial processes. They might, for example, be useful in producing enzymes for accelerating chemical reactions under high-pressure and low-temperature manufacturing conditions.

Marine biologists are interested in learning about the entire spectrum of species that live in the world ocean, where a constant recycling of life forms goes on. This life-cycle ranges from bacteria which decompose plant and animal remains, to plants which absorb the nutrients released by the bacteria, to animals which feed either on these plants or on other animals. When these animals die, they provide food for the bacteria and the cycle begins again.

The plants that live in the open sea and provide the basis for the entire food chain are called phytoplankton. (Plankton means "wandering," for these plants are subject to currents and tides and have almost no power of movement.) They may be microscopic diatoms whose two-part silica cells divide in reproduction, each half forming a new plant, or dinoflagellates, which use their two flagella, or whips, to propel themselves a short distance. Since all phytoplankton require sunlight to produce food, they must remain in the upper layers of the ocean, and their shape or the secretion of tiny oil droplets increases their ability to float and keep them from sinking to lower depths.

Zooplankton, the next layer in the marine-life cycle, are of two types. Temporary zooplankton are the larvae of animals that become either swimming fish or bottom dwellers such as the squirrelfish and the lobster when they mature; permanent zooplankton are organisms such as copepods, which are often called the insects of the sea because many of their forms have antennae and legs; and crustaceans—animals with crustlike shells, such as shrimps.

Pelagic animals (living in the open ocean) occupy various layers of depth. Surface dwellers (epipelagic) include tuna, swordfish, mantas, and crabs. They live in the upper 1000 feet of the ocean. Middle dwellers (mesopelagic) live in the darker parts of the ocean between 1000 and 3000 feet, where little light penetrates. Since there is less food where there is less light, they may come up closer to the surface at night to feed. Certain species of squid, shrimp, and hatchetfish live at this level. Bathypelagic dwellers live at levels from 2000 to 6000 feet, where the water is as cold as it is in the polar regions. At this depth it is totally dark, and there are no plants for food, so these animals prey on each other. The abyssopelagic zone, below the 6000-foot level, has very little animal life except for some species of squid, octopus, and angler fish.

Any organism that lives on the bottom of the ocean—whether close to shore or in the open ocean—is part of the benthos, a Greek word meaning deep sea. Bottom dwellers, which can't move about very well, include worms and clams, crabs and crawfish, lobsters and starfish.

While many forms of marine life can be seen only with a microscope, trips to an aquarium or museum of natural history show us the larger forms: the sharks, whales, dolphins, and fish. All large swimming animals are called nekton (meaning swimming) and

To feed the killer whale "Namu," Washington State fisheries authorities waived a law prohibiting the use of salmon to feed animals. It's the only food he eats in captivity, and he gobbles 400 pounds of it a day.

most—but not all—are predators. The larger marine mammals are either carnivores (feeding on other animals) or, like the sea cow, herbivores (eating only plants, not animals).

Two large groups of ocean dwellers—the sharks and the mammals, such as whales and dolphins—are worthy of special mention here. Ever since the movie *Jaws*, swimmers and the general public have been increasingly shark-conscious. But most species of sharks, with the exception of a few—such as the great white shark and the hammerhead shark—are usually unaggressive toward human beings.

Instead of the bony skeleton that most fish have, the shark's interior framework is made up of cartilage that is usually softer and more flexible than bone. In addition to their well-developed jaws, sharks have five to seven gill openings on each side of the head, and they can protect their eyes from physical or chemical irritants by an opaque membrane that covers the eyeball. Sharks live in all the oceans, although most are found in tropical areas. They vary in length from one foot to forty feet, depending on their species. Marine biologists have discovered that sharks have the highest sensitivity of any animal to electrical fields. This helps them find hidden prey and may also let them orient themselves in the open sea by relating their position to the earth's magnetic field.

Whereas the shark is a fish, a whale is a mammal. Mammals are those species of higher vertebrates that, like human beings, nourish their young with milk secreted by mammary glands. Mammals such as whales, dolphins, and porpoises are known as cetaceans and are thought to be land dwellers who returned to the sea. Since mammals breathe air, they come to the surface to take in and expel air from their lungs. Because of their body chemistry, some whales can stay submerged from one to two hours on the air they take in at the surface. Other marine mammals, like the sea otter or sea lion, may spend more time out of the water.

58

Some species of whales and manatees, the sea cows that some early sailors thought were mermaids, are endangered. The United States Fish and Wildlife Service estimates that there are only about 1000 manatees of the Florida species now. They are found from the North Carolina coast to the Texas Gulf in the summer, but mostly stay in Florida waters during the winter. Other species of sea cows live in the coastal waters of the Red Sea, the Indian Ocean, and other tropical seas.

The wholesale depletion of whales by the whaling industry after the development of factory ships in the twentieth century forced the establishment of the International Whaling Commission. This group attempts to regulate the catch through agreements among the primary whaling countries: Brazil, Chile, Denmark, Iceland, Japan, Korea, Norway, Peru, Spain, and the USSR. Enforcement is rarely possible, however, since many ships do not adhere to the commission's regulations.

Because some species of whales are endangered, much research must still be done in whale biology: we need to learn how and where they breed, their distribution, their life-cycles, and many other aspects of their behavior.

Fish have brains and nervous systems, and some species have a highly developed sense of vision or smell that helps them adapt to their environment. Marine mammals such as whales, porpoises, and dolphins have the most well-developed brains. This is one reason why dolphins are popular at aquatic shows. Their aptitude for learning has also prompted the United States Navy to use them to locate sonar targets or participate in research experiments. Some researchers are also considering whether they would be useful as aquatic "cowboys" in ocean "ranches" to herd fish into specific grazing areas and then, on command from electronic devices attached to their bodies, to guide the fish into corrals for harvesting.

But it is the gregariousness of dolphins—their eagerness to

This porpoise named "Tuffy" is shown taking a line from an experimental diver rescue reel to a diver. This system was developed to aid divers who are disoriented and might otherwise be in serious trouble.

relate to human beings—that makes them so appealing. They have qualities that resemble the best aspects of our nature: a sense of fun and playing games just for the enjoyment of it, for example, and they have been known to help people in trouble in the water. Many stories have been told of how they have kept swimmers from approaching dangerous waters or steered them to shallower waters.

Although the majority of ocean plants are planktonic—those single-celled organisms, described earlier, that float in the sea and are eaten by zooplankton—there are several other types. Algae, some forms of which we see as slimy green scum on ponds, may be either minute floating forms or huge plants attached to the sea bottom and growing 100 feet high, as in the case of some forms of seaweed. Algae are a form of plant known as thallophyta. The only other plant forms found in the ocean are spermatophyta—seed-bearing, flowering plants. These belong among the highest forms of plant life, and scientists believe they did not originate in the ocean but entered it from land or fresh water. Very few species of spermatophyta are found in the ocean, but one that is important is zostera, whose very long narrow leaves are called eelgrass. Where it grows thickly, it provides a hiding place from predators for various forms of marine life.

Most scientists believe that life first began in the sea. The plants and animals we see now, they say, are evolved species of much more primitive forms, the fossils of which we may find today. The fact that there are similar species of fishes, insects, birds, and mammals in widely separated parts of the globe has given rise to two conflicting theories. One group of scientists, the dispersalists, says the species simply spread out from a central point of origin, carried by wind or sea or the search for a better land environment. The other group, whose theory is called vicariance biogeography, suggests that they were separated by the movements of the earth's crust, which thrust up mountains or created oceans where there were none before.

The research of many marine biologists focuses on finding out which species of marine life live, breed, and die at which levels of the ocean. One such study, conducted by a zooplankton ecologist, concentrates on the feeding ecology of the small crustaceans that live in the upper three thousand feet of the ocean. Gathering samples from the sea and then studying them in the laboratory (sometimes with videotape and computer as well as microscope) helps determine, for example, the egg-production rates of these organisms and how that might be affected by the presence of oil in the water. If we want to know how much food from marine life is available to us, we need to know what kind of food these marine creatures themselves need, how each organism breeds, and how their life processes are affected by substances found in seawater.

Other research studies and classifies the fishes of the western North Atlantic. By the use of nets, echo sounders, submersible vehicles, and cameras, enough facts have been gathered to divide the Atlantic into regions based on the distribution patterns of its fishes.

Nations that need fish for their human populations, fish meal to feed poultry and livestock, or other fish products must know which species can be located in which parts of the ocean, and whether they remain in well-defined areas or migrate.

A major question is what causes some species of marine life to evolve and others to disappear. A study of nautiluses—the shelled cephalopods that live 1500 or more feet below the surface—produced a theory that most of the ancestors of the few species of nautiluses that still exist died out 300 million years ago, when fish evolved and could swim faster in search of food than could their clumsy, shelled neighbors. The nautiluses that survived fled to deeper water, where there was less competition and where they could scavenge the debris of dead creatures floating down from above. Some scientists believe that the form into which a creature evolves will determine its success in surviving changes in the competitive environment. For example, the squid and the octopus, two types of cephalopods that abandoned their shells, still prosper today.

Research on marine life-processes can also tell us about our own bodies and how to achieve longer, healthier lives. For example, scientists discovered an anticancer agent that occurs in the livers of certain clams. An extract of this, called mercenene by one of the scientists after the species of clam, has worked effectively as an anticancer agent in mice, as was confirmed by nineteen independent investigators. Research is being conducted on the wound-healing applications of microcrystalline chitin (chitin is a substance that forms part of the outer shell of crustaceans and insects).

Other researchers are investigating the toxins by which certain fish protect themselves from attack by predators. The fluids they eject affect the predators' nervous systems. For example, the Red Sea Moses sole, a bottom-dwelling fish, secretes a milky substance that keeps its predator, a species of shark, away for hours. Only when the sole runs out of its poison will the shark attack. Scientists have been studying toxins and their possible use in treating disorders such as schizophrenia; Alzheimer's Disease, which is a form of dementia; and the nervous disorder called Lou Gehrig's disease. They hope that the toxins might be used to "disconnect" the body's normal nervous system and thus enable them to study and repair or prevent nervous system disorders.

Nonscientists of all ages who are interested in the work of oceanographers and marine biologists have an opportunity to participate in field research through organizations such as Earthwatch, located in Belmont, Massachusetts, and founded in 1971 as a national volunteer organization. Persons who are willing to pay a fee to accompany scientists on a two- or three-week expedition can do much of the information gathering and help defray the costs of research. For example, Rosanne Bonjouklian, whose regular job is senior organic chemist with the Lilly Research Laboratories in Indianapolis, writes: "I love the ocean, beachcombing, snorkeling, and am interested in learning how marine scientists carry out their experiments. On a 'Life on the Rocks' Earthwatch trip to the Bermuda Biological Research Station led by Dr. Susan Cook, a marine zoologist from Ohio State, we studied the pulmonate limpet. We were at the water's edge all the time—but especially at the periods from 6:30 to 8:30 A.M. and 12 to 1 P.M., when the tides were moving in and out at their apex. [The limpet, a delicate flat snail, must venture out daily from its sanctuary in the sheltered depressions of rocks, braving the powerful tidal swells, to search for the algae which constitute its food.] We measured and marked individual limpets, found egg masses, and counted eggs in sections of the masses, using the microscope. We photographed and made maps of limpet movements. On the limpet program I gained a stronger feeling for the harsh environments that nature can provide, for life and death. When you've watched the same limpets for days, and then, on the next, they've been washed away and then found dead in a stagnant tidal pool, you feel a loss."

Marine biologist Dr. Sylvia Earle made her solo record-breaking dive to 1,250 feet in a Jim Suit like this. Its metal shell protects the diver from intense deep-water pressure.

(right)
Natural gas which has accumulated in traps under the earth is tapped by production wells like this one in the Gulf of Mexico.

(below)
Supertankers are economical transporters of oil, but are often too big to maneuver close to harbor unloading facilities, making it necessary to unload cargo to smaller vessels.

(left)
Called "Guppy" because of its small fish-like shape, this Deep Submergence Research Vehicle is used to probe the riches of the sea.

(below)
When this tanker grounded on the northern coast of France in 1978, its spilled oil threatened not only the tourist beaches but the fisheries of the Breton coast as well.

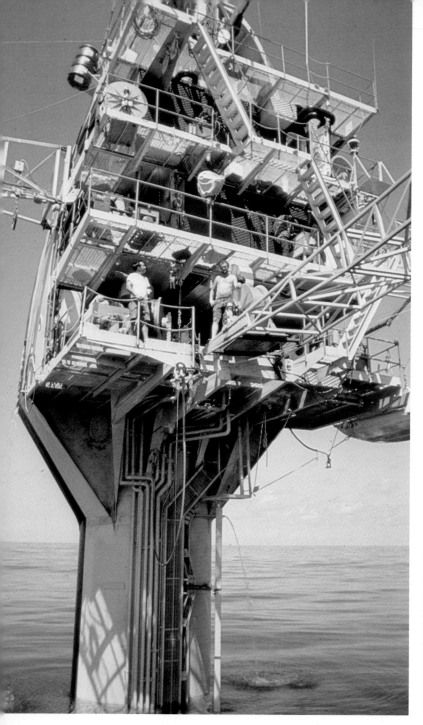

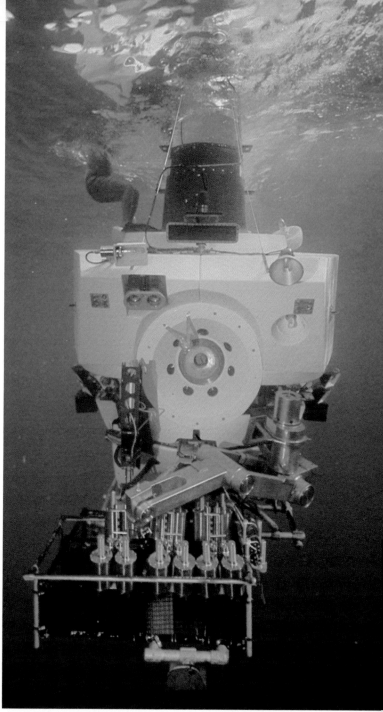

This Floating Instrument Platform (FLIP) is used to measure sound and energy waves at sea. Its 355-foot-long hull is towed to the research site, the ballast tanks are flooded, and the vessel "flips" upright for a stable research vessel.

Among the most versatile tools for oceanographic research is the Deep Submergence Research Vehicle *Alvin* of the Woods Hole Oceanographic Institution. Its special equipment includes rock drills, a magnetometer, a gravimeter, a plankton recorder and sophisticated water sampling devices.

Students on an Oceanic Society expedition use a trawl to bring up an otter.

Before the Food and Agriculture Organization of the United Nations helped developing coastal countries to create and manage their own fisheries, they lost most of the catch off their shores to foreign fishing vessels.

Sea otters help maintain the ecological balance
in kelp beds by feeding on sea urchins, which
feed on kelp.

(left)
This parrotfish peering warily at the photographer from a coral reef is just one of 20,000 species of fish that lend their color and graceful movement to the underwater world.

(right)
More and more women scientists like this female aquanaut are involved in the underwater research of marine biology.

(right)
As much as 20% of some Far Eastern countries' diets come from seaweed such as this harvested by a Japanese seafarmer.

(below)
Land and sea may meet at a gentle sweep of sandy beach or a harsh outcropping of rock, as here on the California coastline.

5

HARVESTS FROM THE SEA

The ocean yields several kinds of "harvests": seaweed, used both for food and in industry; minerals such as iodine; and—more exotically—sunken treasure.

It's hard to imagine a time when human beings didn't know that they could live on the meat of fish caught by hand or, later, with primitive spears and hooks. But once that source was discovered, people who lived near rivers, lakes, seas, and oceans had what seemed an inexhaustible food supply.

Most of the fish we eat, and the plants and other animals *they* eat, live in the upper layer of the ocean, which is warmed by the sun's rays. The area where this warm water meets the deeper cold water is called the thermocline. One of the reasons marine biologists study the oceans is to determine where the water temperature, nutrients, and other factors create the ideal conditions for the presence of harvestable fish stocks.

Satellite sensing of the oceans helps scientists locate likely fishing grounds through computer-enhanced color images of the chlorophyll in the water. Modern techniques for locating fish also include the use of helicopters, submersible vehicles, and sonar. But the majority of research is conducted by taking worldwide water samplings to test for the nutrients that must be there as part of the food chain. (The food chain is a circle of life in which mineral nutrients in the sea are absorbed by plants that feed fish that in turn are eaten by human beings.) For ocean plants to grow, they need not only sunlight but oxygen and carbon dioxide and the nitrogen and phosphorus from decayed organic material as well.

An important part of food-chain research is centered on "up-wellings"—those portions of the ocean in which the vertical movements of the sea bring up rich waters from below, where nutrients exist, to the warm upper layers to provide fertilizer for phytoplankton and other marine life. Upwellings off the coast of Peru help make that country one of the world's leading fishing nations (the others are Japan, China, the Soviet Union, Norway, and the United States). Peru's catch is primarily sardines, herring, and anchovies. But every so often, the phenomenon called El Niño (meaning "the Child," because it often occurs around Christmastime) painfully reminds Peru that nature, not human beings, makes the rules. Normally Peru's strong northerly current pushes out to sea, bringing with it an upwelling of rich nutrients. But occasionally a combination of weak coastal winds and an abnormal surge of warm water moving southward down the coastline prevents the upwelling. Then the phytoplankton cannot reproduce in sufficient quantity to supply the anchovies, which normally feed on them, and the anchovies die out.

Depending on the type of fish and the depths at which they are found, there are two types of commercial fishing. Those fish that are caught by means of drift nets and lines (pelagic fishing) include mackerel and herring, which live in the open ocean. Fish from deeper water such as flounder, which feed on bottom-dwelling

66

invertebrates, are caught by trawl nets or handlines operated from the ship's deck (demersal fishing).

While the development of certain fish-catching technologies—hydraulic-power blocks for pulling in bigger and bigger nets, and sonar and echo sounders both for locating schools of fish and then for telling when the net is full—has increased the number of fish caught, it has also resulted in the periodic overharvesting of some fishes such as herring and mackerel. Major fishing nations such as Japan and the Soviet Union have also built huge factory ships that can stay at sea for long periods and which can quick-freeze or process the catch as it occurs. This, too, has helped to deplete the stock of fish in the world's oceans.

A Maine fisherman hauls in a bountiful catch off the Grand Banks, a submarine plateau off the coast of Canada.

Both technology and governmental regulations have forced changes in net designs. Synthetic fibers have replaced natural ones, reducing breakage and ensuring longer durability. (Can you imagine how fishermen who have put in a hard day's work must feel when they pull in a net and find that it has ripped and that all the fish have escaped?) The size of the mesh in nets has been regulated as well to allow smaller, less mature fish to escape or, in the case of tuna fishing, to keep porpoises from being killed or injured when they become trapped in nets intended for tuna.

The world currently obtains only about 6 percent of its protein from the sea, but the sea has the potential for providing much more. For this reason, researchers are trying to discover how to efficiently harvest new species that would provide not only the fish meal that we feed to poultry and other sources of meat, but also fish and other marine life as a protein-rich food to be eaten directly by human beings.

One method of increasing food supplies is "farming" the sea—a technique that has been used for centuries. For example, a baby oyster floats with the ocean currents until it bumps up against a shell on the bottom to which it can attach itself. Oyster fishermen therefore cluster shells in appropriate areas in order to attract oysters. Then all they need to do is go to that site and "harvest" the oysters. A refinement on this technique is to string shells vertically in the water so that more oysters can be grown in a given area. Today, oysters, mussels, clams, and scallops are harvested in Japan, China, and elsewhere from these controlled beds.

Shrimp are a popular export food. In Ecuador, 75 percent of the shrimp production comes from manmade ponds. One of the largest covers forty-four acres at Guayaquil. Wild adult shrimp are taken from the Pacific and then bred under laboratory conditions. These female shrimp can produce up to a total of 600,000 eggs in their three spawning periods. After a twelve-day, three-stage pro-

Aquaculture in controlled beds like these increases production of shellfish. Vertical strings of shells are lowered into ocean estuaries to provide settlement sites for the larvae of mollusks such as oysters.

cess, larvae are placed in a juvenile pond, then in an adult pond. The ponds are fed by ocean water through a canal. A mesh screen keeps out predators. After harvesting, the pond is drained and cleaned, seeded to create a new organic bottom, then refilled with new larvae.

The term "ocean ranching" was first applied to salmon, which feed and grow in the ocean and then return to rivers to spawn. In the normal course of events, the females swim up these rivers to lay their eggs. But hatcheries had to be built when their natural spawning beds were blocked or eliminated by dams or other obstructions. Eggs from females fertilized by the sperm of adult males returned from the ocean are hatched and the young are raised in these hatcheries until they are ready for their migration to the sea, at which time they are released. This system helps increase the population of salmon, which are then caught by fishermen. The United States, Japan, and the Soviet Union are major ocean-ranching nations. Each year, the Japanese release one billion and the Soviets 800 million salmon from their hatcheries. Hatcheries along America's Pacific Coast release about 400 million.

Experiments are also being conducted with sewage effluent, the water of which contains a source of nutrients for phytoplankton. Phytoplankton are then fed to oysters, mussels, and clams. Solid waste products from these, in turn, are eaten by worms and other small marine animals. Liquid wastes are absorbed by seaweed.

Several conditions point to the possible increase in aquaculture, as sea farming is called. First, fish living in the open sea lay thousands of eggs because so few of them normally survive. But when the fish are raised in controlled areas, the percentage of marketable adults increases considerably. Second, the price of oil to operate fishing fleets makes aquaculture one economic alternative to fishing in the open sea for the harvest of food from the sea.

On the other hand, the cost of aquaculture is such that it would make sense to use it only for the production of the kinds of fish that the world market will purchase and eat. Getting any nation or group of nations to switch its eating habits usually requires economic necessity. For example, when California abalone became scarce because of overfishing and the recent federal protection of sea otters, which have an enormous appetite for abalone, some West Coast restaurant owners began to substitute squid on their menus in an attempt to convert customers to this similar-tasting food. Since Americans have a sea-monster image of the squid, with its tentacles and ink-shooting defenses, some restaurateurs promoted it instead by its Italian name, calamari, and by proper preparation they avoided the toughness objected to by some diners. Squid and shark are eaten in other parts of the world, but haven't been popular in the United States. Another fish product that has not found acceptance with American consumers is fish-protein concentrate (FPC), a tasteless, odorless, cheap flour made from processed fish. Even though there is no taste of fish and the concentrate is a good source of protein, it has not been accepted in the

70

United States, where other sources of protein are readily available.

Half of the world's population, it is estimated, has a diet deficient in protein, and some underdeveloped countries are growing faster than their food supply. Yet we commercially exploit only about fifteen of the 20,000 known marine species. One-third of the world's fish catch is not eaten directly by human beings but is processed into fertilizers and/or used for animal and poultry feeds. As we dangerously approach upsetting the balance between growth and catch rates of the fish we now use, fisheries scientists are studying the areas of the ocean where phytoplankton provide the base of the food chain for the zooplankton, which are then eaten by fish. They are also studying the breeding rates and behavior of those species that might be successfully added to our direct food supply.

Also, as world population grows—especially in nations that depend heavily on oceans for a large part of their diet—the scramble for the available resources increases. There is a constant battle being waged between marine biologists and fisheries over the maximum number of fish that can be taken from the known fishing grounds without destroying the growth/catch balance. International quotas have had to be established for some overfished species.

Statistics on overfishing are chilling. From time to time, herring have been depleted from the Baltic, yellowtail flounder from Alaskan waters, and haddock from the Georges Bank off the New England coast.

Some fishing nations switch to other types of fish to permit the declining species to replenish themselves, but not all have been willing to sign the agreements that limit catches of certain species, and enforcement of these agreements is difficult if not impossible.

The Law of the Sea Treaty Conference is one attempt to gain worldwide cooperation in managing the resources of the food supply in the sea. This management applies not only to fish that breed and live in specific locations, but to migratory species such as the tuna; to anadromous species such as the salmon, which lives in the ocean but returns to fresh water to spawn; and to catadromous fish such as eels, which are hatched in the sea and live in fresh water.

The world fish catch today is about seventy million metric tons per year. By the year 2000, U.N. forecasters expect fisheries to catch between 100 and 150 million tons. This means that international cooperation is vital if we are to maintain a balance between how many fish live in the ocean and how many are caught.

Marine life consists of plants as well as animals, and one of the plants most aggressively investigated for its uses today is seaweed. For the Japanese, Burmese, Russians, and Chinese, seaweed is a food. It is harvested off the coasts of the United States for other purposes. From the species in New England called Irish moss is extracted a substance called carrageen. From California kelp is extracted an essence called algin. These substances are present as stabilizers or emulsifiers in hundreds of products we use every day. Algin, for example, is what helps keep ice cream smooth, stabilizes the foam on beer, keeps the chocolate in chocolate milk from set-

With the establishment of Exclusive Economic Zones, and the help of the United Nations, coastal developing nations have been able to catch and process more of their own resources, as in this fish freezing and processing plant in Dakar, West Africa.

tling to the bottom, and stabilizes pulp and concentrates in fruit juices. It is also used in industrial products such as polishes, paints, and plasters, and in textile printing processes. Carrageen is used as a stabilizer too, but primarily in foods and toothpastes.

Kelp is harvested from underwater forests off the California coast. Like all marine life, it is dependent upon its ocean environment. In the late 1950s, many California kelp forests were dwindling and on the verge of being lost: exceptionally warm ocean waters were killing the giant plants. In addition, they were being destroyed by sea urchins, a spiny marine animal that feeds on kelp, and whose own natural enemy, the sea otter, had been overhunted, upsetting the ecological balance of the kelp beds. But when the water temperature returned to a more normal level and sea urchins were controlled by the return of the sea otter, the kelp forests regrew. Ships with special cutting blades were again able to harvest bountiful supplies of kelp.

As already mentioned, we harvest more than fish and plants from the sea. Of the presently known oil reserves, 37 percent, or an estimated 240 billion barrels, lies offshore. The ocean also has rich deposits of natural gas and manganese nodules containing manganese, copper, nickel, cobalt, and molybdenum.

Seawater itself is a mineral resource. Approximately sixty nations process it to obtain magnesium, iodine, calcium, bromine, and potassium. An important product of the evaporation of seawater is table salt. The United States produces over 1.5 million tons of salt a year by this method.

Oyster shells are one ingredient of the limestone from which cement is made, and each year more than fifty million tons of sand and gravel are taken from the ocean for construction purposes.

Sulfur is one of the byproducts of the oil- and gas-drilling operations in some areas, and two such locations near the Mississippi Delta produce 15 percent of the sulfur used by the United States.

Some South African rivers that flow into the ocean carry diamonds with them. These are mined off the sea floor and used for both decorative and industrial purposes.

Gold, silver, and other treasures are also "harvested" from the sea, but they got there because of catastrophe—the ships carrying them sank for one reason or another. For years people have been trying to reach these ships in order to retrieve their riches. Salvager Burt Webber and his group, Sea Quest International, did just that in 1979, when they found the seventeenth-century Spanish treasure galleon *Conceptión* off the coast of Santo Domingo. It had been wrecked on a reef in 1641, and although an English expedition took some 68,000 pounds of silver from the vessel in 1687, about a thousand coins and other gold and silver objects remained on the wreck almost 300 years before being rediscovered. The value of the total find is estimated at $40 million. This amount is to be split between Santo Domingo (51 percent) and Sea Quest (49 percent).

One of the most recent recoveries from a sunken gold-laden ship was the 1981 work of divers in the icy Barents Sea in the Arctic, 170 miles north of Murmansk. They were seeking the gold on the British cruiser H.M.S. *Edinburgh,* which had been attacked by a Nazi submarine and was sunk in 1942 by the British themselves to keep the Germans from getting the gold. The *Edinburgh* had been bearing gold to the United States in payment for military supplies. The gold was originally part of the Russian imperial treasury taken over by the Bolsheviks in 1917. The *Edinburgh* was carrying the gold as the command ship of a thirteen-vessel convoy of ships belonging to the countries allied against Germany. The five tons of gold ingots, stamped with the double-headed eagle of the czars of Russia, was valued at $8.9 million at the time they were lost—at today's gold prices the figure is closer to $80 million. The United States government was paid by an insurance settlement when the ship sank. Therefore, the gold is being split according to

an agreement between the salvage crew (45 percent) and the Soviet and British governments (two thirds and one third, respectively, of the balance). Keith Jessup of Britain, who organized the expedition, spent $4 million and two years locating the wreck and diving into the 800-foot-deep icy water. The divers, veterans of Britain's treacherous North Sea oil fields, had to cut through the *Edinburgh*'s fuel tanks to get at the gold, which was stored in the strongroom wedged between two weapon holds.

The current project of Britain's salvage crews is not a search for gold but the raising, restoring and display of the *Mary Rose*, King Henry VIII's warship which was sunk off Portsmouth, England, in 1545. Before the hull itself was raised, divers had brought up thousands of artifacts that give us a better picture of what kinds of longbows, navigation instruments, coins, and food and drink utensils were a part of sixteenth-century English life.

Among the 16th-century artifacts retrieved from the *Mary Rose* in Portsmouth harbor by English divers was this ship's compass.

Not all shipwrecks contain valuable cargo, but those that do inevitably lure the adventurer, the speculator, and the investor. It has been more than seventy years since the *Titanic*, meant to be the first "unsinkable" ship, hit an iceberg April 14, 1912, and went to the bottom with three-quarters of its 2000 passengers. Now a Texas millionaire says he will try to see, at his own expense, what riches that famous ship will yield to undersea explorers.

6

POLLUTION OF THE SEA

The ocean has always seemed limitless in its ability to absorb what pours, flows, or seeps into it, so that we have only recently begun to question how much waste and refuse it can take without irreversible harm.

There are five actual or potential sources of marine pollution, of which land-based activities account for about 90 percent. This pollution comes from factories, sewage, and anything else people put directly into rivers or atmosphere and then into the oceans. The other four causes are pollution from vessels, continental shelf drilling, deep-seabed mining, and ocean dumping.

Eugene Smith's heartrending photographs of the victims of mercury poisoning in Japan's Minimata Bay showed us the dangers of industrial dumping of heavy waste metals such as mercury, nickel, and lead into the sea. Many organisms can take in high concentrations of waste metals and not be affected by them. However, if these organisms are in turn eaten by human beings, the results can be dangerous—even deadly.

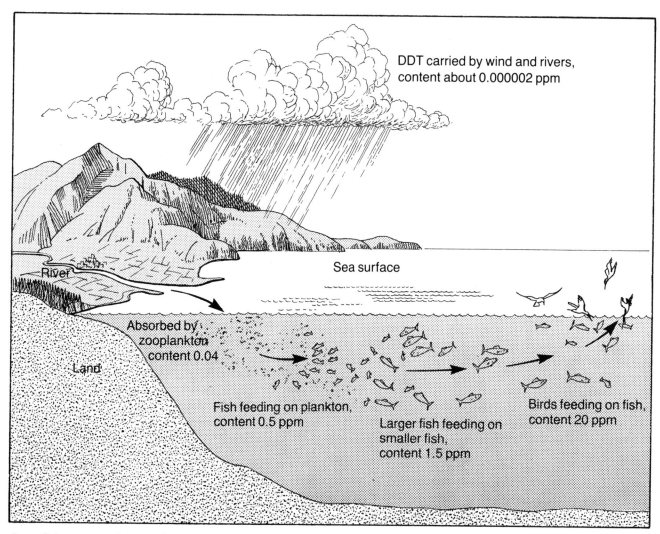

DDT carried by wind and rivers, content about 0.000002 ppm

Sea surface

River

Land

Absorbed by zooplankton content 0.04

Fish feeding on plankton, content 0.5 ppm

Larger fish feeding on smaller fish, content 1.5 ppm

Birds feeding on fish, content 20 ppm

One of the reasons the use of DDT is now restricted is that even though its initial spraying uses only a small number of parts per million, it collects and rises to a dangerous level in the fish we may eat. (Rendering after a diagram in *Opportunities and Uses of the Ocean* by David Ross.)

Some of the problems associated with pollutants are related to the balance of oxygen in the water. Certain nutrients are critical for plant growth, but if, for example, in a coastal area where large amounts of wastes containing nutrients such as phosphorous and nitrogen empty into the water, the growth of phytoplankton may increase to such a point that when they decay, they use up all the available oxygen in the water, leaving none for fish and other forms of aquatic life. In addition to causing oxygen depletion, increased nutrient supplies from pollution may also lead to the growth of undesired species close to shore. An example of this is the "red tide," which appears along the Florida Gulf Coast almost every year. Red tides are caused by the rapid growth of a certain species of phytoplankton that gives the water a reddish cast. These phytoplankton are generally not poisonous to the fish, mussels, and clams that feed on them, but can be fatal to the human beings who consume the fish and shellfish.

Another concern of marine scientists is the synthetic organic compound wastes that come from petrochemical and other factories. Many of these compounds do not break down very quickly, and tests have shown that polychlorinated biphenyls (PCBs) have reduced the growth rate of phytoplankton even when present in concentrations as low as ten parts per billion. And whatever affects phytoplankton also affects us human beings as the ultimate members of the food chain, since we eat the fish that eat the plankton.

One of the ways scientists have been able to monitor pollution along both coasts of the United States is called Mussel Watch. Since the blue-black bivalve mussel known as mytilus processes up to two quarts of seawater an hour over its gills to extract oxygen and nutrients, it also filters any contaminants in the water at the same time. By chemically analyzing the flesh of mussels gathered from the shoreline, scientists discovered plutonium off Plymouth, Massachusetts, near a nuclear plant; PCBs in the harbor at New Bedford, Massachusetts; and DDT that was still in the water off southern California five years after the pesticide was banned. Pesticides and PCBs are now found in all the wilderness—even in Antarctic regions.

The success of Mussel Watch in the United States prompted the United Nations to adopt the same method to help track pollution in the Mediterranean. Since nearly 90 percent of the sewage that pours into the Mediterranean is untreated, pollution in this area had caused outbreaks of cholera and typhoid among people who live or work along its shores. The United Nations Environment Program funded a pollution-monitoring system of over eighty laboratories to check on water conditions and was able to get the cooperation of seventeen nations bordering the Mediterranean to approve a treaty outlining ways to clean it up. Since the Mediterranean is a vacation spot for 100 million tourists a year, the cost of antipollution efforts is an economic as well as a health necessity.

In the United States, the Coast Guard maintains a twenty-four-hour National Response Center pollution watch hotline so that any oil, gasoline, or chemical spills can be reported. That holds true not only for the tanker that goes aground but for the recreational houseboater who accidentally drops a can of paint overboard. Reports to this hotline, (800) 424-8802, should provide the duty officer with the cause, location, kind, and time of any spills plus, of course, description of any injuries. In the case of large spills, once they are analyzed, a private company contracts to do the work. Special equipment includes absorbent mats, mops, skimmers, and booms that keep the spill from spreading as well as large vacuums that suck the pollutant out of the water. Major oil spills may take a week or more to clean up; chemical spills can be more difficult and more expensive, if indeed they can be cleaned up at all.

The problem of pollution from ships on the high seas has been a concern of the Law of the Sea Treaty Conference. It is trying to

get international agreement on how ships could be more safely designed and what maximum levels of pollution discharge should be allowed. The grounded wrecks of the *Torrey Canyon* off Cornwall, England, in 1967 and the *Amoco Cadiz* off northern France in 1978 (in which 100,000 and 220,000 tons, respectively, of oil spilled into the sea and spoiled nearby beaches) dramatically made the public aware of oil pollution. But a much greater quantity of oil enters the sea as a result of normal tanker operations. An oil tanker carries its cargo in a number of tanks or compartments within the hull. After the oil is discharged, about one-third of the tanks have to be filled with seawater so that the ship's propeller is properly immersed and the ship has the correct handling characteristics. This process is known as ballasting. Once the ballast voyage is under way, approximately half of the remaining tanks must be cleaned of the oil residues, which cling to the sides and bottoms of the tanks once the oil has been discharged. In the early days of

When the oil tanker *Amoco Cadiz* grounded off the coast of Brittany in 1978, 220,000 tons of crude oil spilled into the sea. Soldiers and volunteers stemmed the progress of the "Black Tide" with this rubber flotation barrier.

81

tanker operations, it was common practice to clear tanks by spraying seawater into them with jets. The mixture of oil and water collected at the bottom of the tanks was then pumped overboard.

To address such problems as these, the Inter-Governmental Maritime Consultive Organization (IGMCO) was formed in 1948. A specialized agency of the United Nations, its main objectives are to improve safety at sea and prevent marine pollution from ships.

Operational techniques developed by industry during the 1960s provided a method which would eliminate this source of operational pollution. The system known as "load on top" was created in which the oil-water mixtures resulting from tank-cleaning operations are pumped into a special slop tank on board the ship. During the course of the voyage, the oil and water separate: the oil floats to the top of the tank, making it possible to pump the clean water below into the while the floating oil remains in the slop tank. At the loading port, new oil is loaded on top of the residual oil in the slop tank. The IGMCO, which changed its name in 1982 to The International Maritime Organization (IMO), has also set standards for the design and construction of ships as well as for maximum permissible levels of pollution discharge that will be acceptable to every nation.

As more and more offshore drilling exploration continues, the responsibilities of coastal countries for preventing marine pollution increase; and if deep-seabed mining becomes a reality, the International Seabed Authority will have the duty to both prescribe and enforce antipollution measures in that area.

In December 1981, for example, the national Center for Disease Control in Atlanta, Georgia, pointed out that untreated sewage illegally dumped from a Texas oil well worksite had led to the largest outbreak of cholera in the United States in the twentieth century. The oil well was drilled in a freshwater-lake region along the Texas coastline, and the outbreak occurred because untreated sewage was dumped through an outflow pipe that was close to the drilling rig's freshwater intake pipe. The primary dangers of pollution from offshore drilling, however, are from operations where adequate safety precautions are not taken. The blowout in Mexico's Campeche oil field in 1979 spewed millions of gallons of oil for several months into the Gulf of Mexico before the flow could be cut off.

In 1972 the London Dumping Convention was created as an international means to try to control or prohibit the dumping of all radioactive waste and other harmful materials into the ocean. The U.S. Navy, for example, has five old nuclear-powered submarines waiting for burial. One option is to take the nuclear fuel out and then dump the ships in the deep parts of the Atlantic or Pacific. In the past, low-level radioactive wastes from the world's nuclear reactors have often been put in drums enclosed in concrete that would be resistant to water pressure and sunk in the ocean.

Pollution enters the ocean from the atmosphere as well as from material dumped into it, so protection of every aspect of the global environment is vitally important. The Organization for Economic Cooperation and Development, made up of the major non-Communist industrial nations, has been studying not only hazardous wastes, but also such problems as acid rain produced in the atmosphere from wind-carried outpourings from factory and power plant smokestacks and the effects of carbon dioxide from coal burning heating up the world's climate through a "greenhouse" effect. (Scientists theorize that the buildup of carbon dioxide in the atmosphere captures heat reflected from the earth's surface, preventing the heat from escaping into space. That heat is then returned to earth, raising world temperatures several degrees, the way heat is built up inside a greenhouse.) And there are international agreements to limit atmospheric testing of nuclear bombs.

Since it will take up to a million years to dissipate some forms of radioactivity such as plutonium, the control of its release into the atmosphere and oceans is a continuing international problem. During the fifties and early sixties, atmospheric testing released many artificial radionuclides into the atmosphere and thence to the oceans. We can still trace these in the oceans today. Although the levels are not higher in seawater, they can be "concentrated" by organisms, which absorb them and which if eaten would be highly toxic to human beings. Continued work on reactors and fuel reprocessing means some radionuclides continue to be added to the oceans today.

We don't normally think of salt as pollution, but in the sense that it keeps seawater from being drinkable, it has that characteristic. As world population increases and the supplies of fresh water fail to keep up with the demand, more and more attention is turning to desalination. This process, by which dissolved salts and other impurities are removed from seawater, can be accomplished in several different ways. More than half of the 1500 world desalting plants that produce 25,000 gallons of fresh water per day or more use the distillation process. In this method, saltwater is boiled and the steam is captured and condensed into fresh water. The other plants primarily use one of several "membrane" processes. In one such technique, saltwater is forced against the membrane under pressure, and water, but not the salts, passes through it. In another, saltwater is put into a container divided into three parts by membranes. Electric current is passed through the container, and charged salt particles move to positive or negative electrical poles at the end sections. The center section is left with fresh water.

Desalting plants located in the Middle East and North Africa produce more than 55 percent of the worldwide plant capacity; Europe and Asia about 25 percent. The United States produces about 10 percent, while the Caribbean and the rest of the world produces the remaining 10 percent.

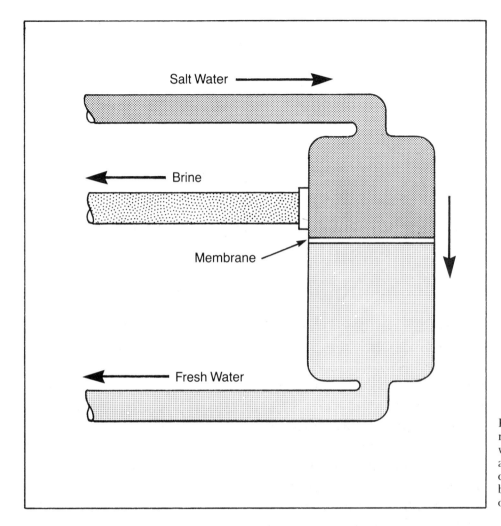

Salt Water →

← Brine

Membrane

← Fresh Water

Reverse osmosis is one technique of desalting water. Saltwater under pressure is forced against a membrane. The salts cannot pass through the membrane, so fresh water appears on the other side.

Natural desalination of seawater—through evaporation, cloud formation, and rain—provides most of our fresh water. But some parts of the world receive little rainfall and others suffer from periodic droughts. Desalination can also be used on brackish inland waters as well as near the ocean and is the hope of many countries facing the problem of less and less natural fresh water in the future.

7

STRAITS AND CANALS

The word "oceans" usually brings to mind the high seas—those limitless expanses where sea meets sky on every horizon and the world seems nothing but water. But oceans also tuck themselves into straits—narrow passageways connecting two large bodies of water. Where a thin strip of land separates two important water bodies, engineers have created canals—artificial passageways used for world shipping.

These narrow waterways are both economically and politically important. Close to 95 percent of the international trade still involves ocean transport, and throughout the years, these passageways have been instrumental in facilitating the passage of cargo ships from one ocean to another. Once the Panama Canal was built, for example, ships sailing from the east to the west coasts of the United States no longer had to go round Cape Horn, the southern tip of South America. This shortened their voyage by about 8000 nautical miles, thus providing faster and safer transport. But these waterways have also been the source of conflict, for example when nations bordering the straits and canals have sought to restrict their use for political, economic, or environmental reasons.

The narrow 50-mile Bering Strait separates the northeastern part of the Soviet Union from Alaska and links the Pacific and Arctic oceans. Anthropologists tell us that the ancestors of Eskimos and Indians—along with bisons, mammoths, and other animals—came to the American continent by way of the Bering Strait between 10,000 and 30,000 years ago. During the Ice Age, the sea level fell by several hundred feet making the strait into a land bridge between the continents. Today, the major migrators in the strait are the gray whales that swim from the Bering Sea to warmer Pacific lagoons off the coast of Baja California to give birth to their calves every fall.

For over a hundred years, engineers and entrepreneurs have been considering ways to bridge or tunnel the Bering Strait in order to permit traffic to move from one continent to the other. A Russo-American telegraph cable was planned in 1865, but the successful transatlantic cable in 1867 scotched that effort. French planners promoted a Trans-Alaska-Siberian Railroad, but couldn't find investors since there was no place to deliver goods or passengers once the train got to the barren, icy, unpopulated land on either side of the strait. The most recent proposal involves the laying of a forty-eight-inch-diameter natural gas pipeline linking the Soviet Union gas fields with the proposed gas line crossing Canada and the United States.

A unique proposal was made in 1956 by a group of Soviet scientists to dam the strait and, in the process, to turn the icy wastes into a "garden spot" of the north. A warmer climate would free the Russian Arctic shoreline of ice and possibly allow the planting of crops. Their plan involved the use of powerful pumps to force water from under the ice-covered Arctic Ocean, over a dam, and into the Pacific. Water from the warmer Atlantic currents would be

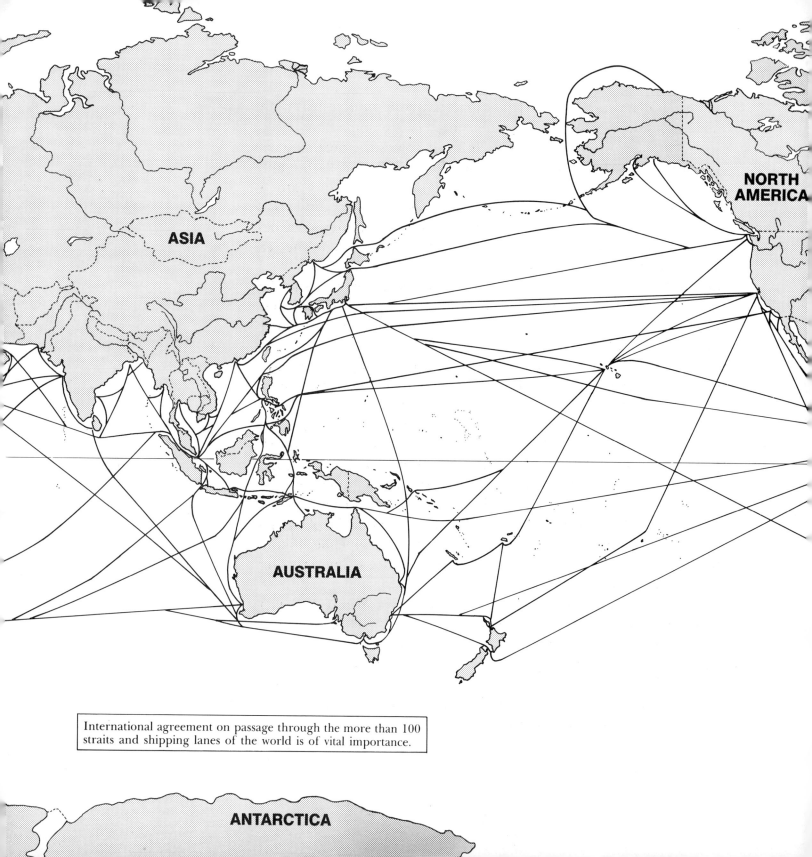

International agreement on passage through the more than 100 straits and shipping lanes of the world is of vital importance.

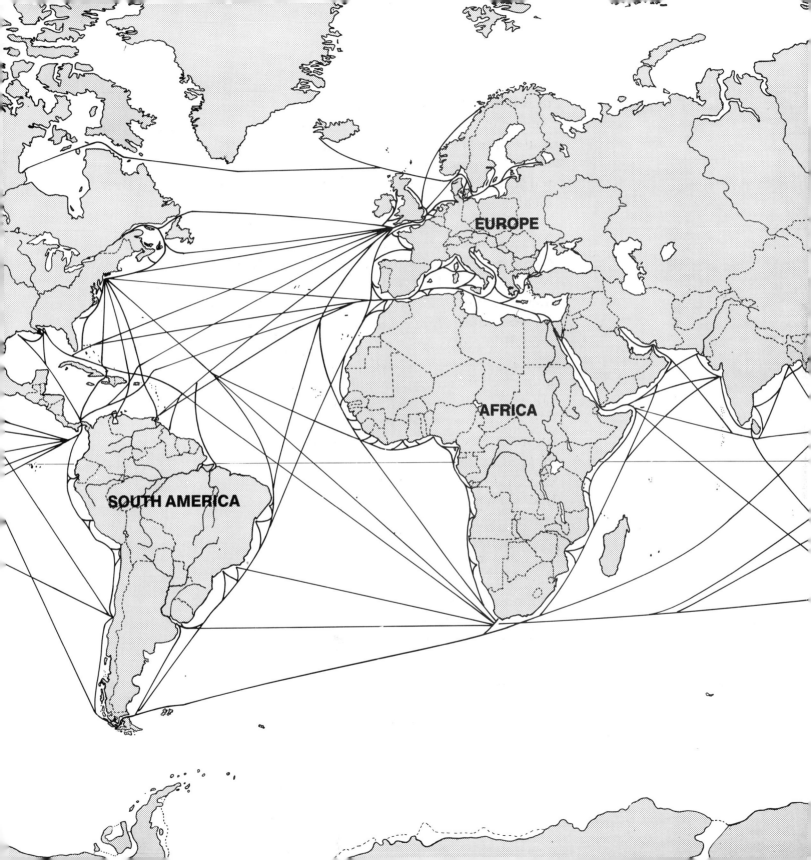

EUROPE

AFRICA

SOUTH AMERICA

drawn into the Arctic, melting the polar ice cap. Other Soviet and American scientists, however, pointed out that such a dam could lead to possible long-term disastrous effects: the chilling of Pacific waters and nearby land area; moderate climates becoming too warm, and the rising sea level inundating coastal cities with the melting ice cap.

The Strait of Gibraltar is the passageway between Spain and Africa, connecting the Atlantic and the Mediterranean. As already mentioned, the heavy evaporation of the Mediterranean, surrounded as it is by warm areas, causes its dense, salty water to sink down and flow out through the strait. At the same time, the lighter surface water of the Atlantic flows into the Mediterranean. Although in olden times this presented problems to westbound sailing ships, which needed a strong tailwind to counteract the inflowing current, it is of no concern to modern ships. The only obstacle to the use of the passageway is a potential military one. The British naval base at Gibraltar, the "Rock" at the southern tip of Spain, is strategically located to control movements of ships in and out of the strait. The naval base is part of the defense alliance operated by the North Atlantic Treaty Organization. The British have been present on Gibraltar since 1704, when they captured this narrow peninsula from Spain during the War of the Spanish Succession, and the Spanish have been trying to get it back ever since. In 1969, General Franco, frustrated in his efforts to reclaim Gibraltar, closed the gates between Spain and Gibraltar, and no automobiles, buses, or trucks could go through. Tourists, for example, who were traveling in southern Spain and wanted to go to Gibraltar, had to take a boat to Morocco and then come back to the Rock, instead of simply riding a few miles farther down the road. Diplomatic negotiations in December 1982 reopened this land border to pedestrians between Gibraltar and Spain and continued in 1983 to determine the citizenship status of the 29,000 inhabitants who voted in a 1967 referendum to remain British subjects.

Probably the most important passageway for the international movement of oil is the Strait of Hormuz, which lies between Iran and Oman on the Arabian peninsula and connects the Persian Gulf with the Gulf of Oman. Prior to the economic downturn in 1980, as much as 50 percent of the free world's oil supply was shipped through this strait. Tankers traveling the sea-lanes between these two bodies of water must keep within two channels, each two miles wide and separated by a 2½-mile-wide safety zone that is maintained between ships traveling east and west to avoid the dangers of collision and the resulting oil spill. The potential danger for disruption of free passage always exists when neighboring coastal states are at war. If that strait were to be closed off by war, only a small portion of the pre-1980 volume of oil passing through the Strait of Hormuz could be accommodated by crude oil pipelines terminating at Mediterranean ports in Syria and Lebanon or at the Saudi Arabian port of Yanbu on the Red Sea. Even portions of some of those pipelines have been subjected to terrorist attacks or government shutdowns in the past.

The most difficult excavating for the Panama Canal was the Gaillard Cut, where the Canal crosses the Continental Divide. Here, the Japanese container ship *Rhine Maru* passes between Contracts Hill and Gold Hill in the Cut.

91

As was mentioned earlier, canals are manmade straits. The Panama Canal connects the Atlantic and Pacific through the Isthmus of Panama and is fifty-one miles long. Inland it is mostly above sea level and needs locks (devices for raising and lowering ships as they travel from one level to another) to raise ships eighty-five feet above sea level at the Atlantic entrance, then lower them thirty-one feet to Lake Miraflores, and finally another fifty-four feet at the Pacific entrance. The principle is the same as the one you may have seen on inland waterways. To pass to a higher level, water in the lock is lowered to the level of the vessel outside; a gate is opened and the ship moves in. After the gate is closed, water enters the lock from the higher level, until water in the lock and outside it are equal. The front gate is then opened and the ship moves out.

The Panama Canal was originally conceived by the French engineer Ferdinand de Lesseps, who had built the Suez Canal. When the French company that started the Panama Canal went bankrupt, its creditors lobbied the United States government to buy the rights to the project. Panama was then part of Colombia. President Theodore Roosevelt and his secretary of state, John Hay, offered $10 million in gold and an annual rent of $250,000. According to the proposed plan, Colombia would retain sovereignty over the canal zone, but the United States could enforce its own regulations. The United States approved the treaty but Colombia rejected it. Subsequently, the province of Panama seceded from Colombia and the United States concluded a treaty with the new state. Since that seemed to violate an earlier agreement guaranteeing the sovereignty of Colombia in the isthmus, the United States in 1921 paid Colombia $25 million as redress for the loss of Panama.

Since October 1, 1979, when the United States government-owned Canal Company, which had operated the canal for seventy-five years, was replaced by another U.S. government agency, the Panama Canal Commission, traffic through the canal has remained steady—about 185 million long tons of cargo pass through annually. (A long ton is 2,240 pounds.) Supertankers, however, are too large to go through the canal, so that oil that might otherwise have been brought down the coast from Alaska and taken through the canal to the East Coast of America will now either have to come by pipeline or be transported in ships small enough to fit the canal.

The present site of the Suez Canal may have been where one of the world's first canals was constructed. As early as 2000 B.C., a canal was dug to Lake Timsah, which was then the north end of the Red Sea. It was extended by Xerxes I, king of Persia, in the fifth century B.C., and then subsequently closed about the eighth century A.D. The present canal is 101 miles long and transverses northeast Egypt and the Sinai between the Mediterranean and the Red seas. It was built in the 1860s by de Lesseps for a British-controlled company. The Suez Canal is a sea-level canal, so, unlike the Panama Canal, it doesn't need locks to take ships through. It is an important trade route between Asia, Africa, and Europe.

With the world depending on oil for 47 percent of its energy, its safe and dependable transport from source to buyer is a major concern. Before the Suez Canal was closed by the war between Israel and Egypt in 1956, an average of only sixty-two oil tankers rounded the Cape of South Africa every month. By 1974 the average was between 500 and 600 a month. The Suez was reopened again in 1980, and the upgraded canal can now handle loaded ships of up to 150,000 tons and ballasted tankers of 375,000 tons. The fully loaded very large crude oil carriers (VLCCs) of over 150,000 tons, however, have too large a draft to use the canal.

Freedom of navigation is now being challenged in many parts of the world where coastal states want to extend their territorial seas. Historically, the distance was about three nautical miles from a coastal nation's shores. Now more than fifty countries claim rights of up to twelve miles. If all nations were to agree to a twelve-mile territorial sea, this would completely overlap more than 100 straits used for international navigation.

Some nations that border straits have sought to restrict the right of navigation to "innocent passage," requiring submarines to travel on the surface and aircraft to receive permission for over-flight. Other nations say this would cause confusion because each nation could interpret "innocent" in a different way. The Third United Nations Law of the Sea Treaty proposes that right of transit be granted to all ships and aircraft in and over straits used for international navigation. There are always exceptions to treaty proposals. In recent years, for example, Egypt refused to let the British nuclear submarine *Dreadnought* pass through the Suez Canal. Egyptian officials pointed out that in case of an accident, nuclear material discharged would be more of a threat in the confined area of the canal than it would be in the open sea.

Maritime nations and those closest to narrow channels are faced with problems that must be solved by mutual agreement. Members of the International Maritime Organization, for example, require oil tankers using the English Channel to navigate in lanes that keep them away from the French coast. In 1978 150 miles of tourist beaches had been blackened by an oil spill from a grounded tanker. Fear of a major pollution accident was also the basis of an earlier agreement between Malaysia and Indonesia involving the Strait of Malacca. Here, the problem was more vital than protecting the tourist trade. Indonesian fishermen depend on the waters around the Indonesian archipelago and the South China Sea for a living, and the pollution of these waters from a tanker spill would have a devastating effect on their livelihood. The international maritime agreement set down designated sea lanes through the Strait of Malacca and also put limits on the draft of supertankers that could pass through it.

Coastal nations want to protect their territorial waters, and the superpowers and other maritime nations want the right of passage for their ships in order to defend their international interests. The Third United Nations Law of the Sea Treaty Conference is attempting to convince all governments to agree on which bodies of water are to be considered straits, which are to be considered international waterways, and what the rules governing the movement of ships through each should be.

8

WHO RULES THE SEAS?

The ship's captain looked up from his chart and glanced at the message brought to him by his first mate while they were in their last port: MARINERS ARE ADVISED TO USE CAUTION WHILE TRANSITING WATERS IN THE APPROACH TO SINGAPORE, AND ESPECIALLY THE STRAIT OF MALACCA IN THE VICINITY OF PHILLIP CHANNEL, BECAUSE OF RECENT ATTACKS ON VESSELS BY PIRATES. A scene on a medieval galley? No, an advisory to international fleet managers from the Maritime Administration in Washington, D.C., dated September 1981.

The channel, thirteen miles south of Singapore, is a very narrow waterway, and when large ships slow down to navigate it, pirates—usually acting at night—use fast motorboats to pull alongside the ships. Using ropes and grappling hooks, they board the ships and rob the captain and crew. For the most part, the pirates want cash, watches, and radios, which they can easily transport in their motorboats. Some of their primary targets have been supertankers because these ride low in the water when fully loaded and, since supertankers are highly automated, they have small unarmed civilian crews. But pirates had other targets in the 1.2 million refugees who fled Vietnam. The United Nations estimates that pirates attacked 25 percent of these boat people, seeking primarily the gold some of them may have taken with them to finance their new lives.

Singapore marine police, together with the Malaysian and Indonesian governments, are trying to cope with the problem, but meantime the ships' captains take their own measures. They find that spraying streams of water from fire hoses can stop the pirates, provided that the night watch discovers the boarding party in time.

Piracy has given rise to some of the earliest laws that govern the activities of men and ships on the sea. In the early days, pirates included not only individuals acting on their own, but also nation-states that robbed one other. One reason Greece and then Rome gained sovereignty over the Mediterranean was their success in suppressing the piracy of less powerful adversaries.

The war against pirates was the origin of the practice, which began in medieval days, of boarding and searching neutral vessels in time of war in order to look for supplies being transported to the enemy. In some cases the next step was to seize the ships if contraband was found on board. "Prize (of war) Courts" were established to settle disputes as to whether captured vessels could be kept legally as a prize of war.

Another aspect of war on the sea was the practice of privateering, by which governments commissioned private vessels to capture enemy shipping. But the practice was used as an excuse for outright piracy, too. Queen Elizabeth I, for example, issued a proclamation in 1602 to stop privateering. It was directed at both her own countrymen and aliens who pretended "to make war against the enemies of her majesty."

In 1981, a modern-day would-be privateer petitioned the United States Congress for a letter of marque (a written authorization to plunder the enemy) such as the one the United States had

Her colors flying in the wind, a British Revenue vessel chases a suspected smuggler ship near Eddystone Lighthouse off the south coast of England.

issued to the pirate/privateer Jean Laffite in the War of 1812, giving permission to attack British ships. The petitioner pointed out that Article I, Section 8 of the Constitution allows Congress to "declare War, grant Letters of Marque and Reprisal and make Rules concerning Captures on Land and Water." This time, the petitioner was a Key West lawyer who wanted to wage war on smugglers, who bring an estimated $7 billion in drugs into Florida from the Caribbean each year. Naturally, the lawyer expected a portion of the value of the take for his services. So far, Congress hasn't decided.

Maritime law has dealt with many other aspects of conduct on the high seas since ancient times. The Mediterranean island of Rhodes is probably best known for its Colossus, the huge bronze statue of the sun god Helios—one of the seven wonders of the ancient world—that straddled the harbor. But this Greek island and early trading center is also famous for one of the first attempts to create laws governing ships and the sea. As early as 900 B.C., Rhodian common law of the sea made provision for payment of salvage awards for goods saved at sea. If a salvager was able to gather up flotsam (ship parts or cargo afloat) or retrieve jetsam (goods cast overboard to lighten it) he would be entitled to one fifth to one tenth of what was saved, depending on the item and depths from which he retrieved it.

Pre-Norman English law, on the other hand, gave to the Crown property of ships that were wrecked along its coastline. Rights of the true owner were considered lapsed by action of the sea. Lords who lived along the seacoast were given "royalty of wreck" from the Crown for their stretch of coastal land. Since Henry II defined a "wreck" as a mishap from which no "man or beast" escaped alive, one shipowner won his suit against a salvage crew because the captain's dog was still alive on board when the crew arrived.

Historians disagree as to who was the first to create a navy and seek dominion over the sea as well as the land. We have colorful stories, for example, of Persian King Xerxes, whose idea to bridge the Hellespont (a strait now known as the Dardanelles) with boats is still copied by modern armies in their use of pontoon bridges. And certainly, as commerce grew up around the settlements in the eastern Mediterranean, Greek and then Roman leaders with fleets of ships proved that "might makes right" in deciding who should control access to certain coasts and harbors. When Roman power declined, however, individual Mediterranean states regained control over areas near their coasts. The Genoese imposed tolls on ships entering the Ligurian Gulf, and Venice controlled the Adriatic.

The Tudors of England, acting under a fourteenth-century Consolato del Mare prize law principle, gave their Admiral of the Fleet instruction to seize any vessels resisting visit and search in British waters.

It was the great voyages of discovery in the fifteenth and sixteenth centuries, however, that set the foundations for modern international law. In 1493, for example, Pope Alexander VI, who was not only a religious figure but a world leader as well, published his famous Bulls (solemn official pronouncements). He divided sovereignty between Spain and Portugal over the then-undiscovered world by a line drawn from pole to pole at a point one hundred leagues west of the Azores. The next year, by a treaty, the rulers of the two nations decided to shift the line to 370 leagues west of the Cape Verde Islands. That shift explains why, to this day, Brazil is Portuguese in background and the rest of South America is Spanish.

Few challenged the claims by Spain and Portugal until the seventeenth century, when the Dutch also wanted to trade with the Indies. The very same Strait of Malacca that was the subject of the warning about modern pirates was the site of a clash between Portuguese and Dutch in 1602. A Dutch East India Company captain had seized a Portuguese galleon in the Strait of Malacca, despite the efforts of both Spain and Portugal to keep the Dutch from trading in both the East and West Indies. The Dutch engaged a young lawyer, Hugo Grotius, to defend their trading policy. He attacked the claims of Spain and Portugal and appealed "to the civilized world for complete freedom of the high seas for the innocent use and mutual benefit of all." He defined property as that which could be occupied, and argued that things that could not be occupied or enclosed should be common to all and their usage for the entire human race rather than for a particular people. This principle was entitled *Mare Liberum,* meaning free sea.

While Holland was proclaiming freedom of the seas with the object of advancing its own commercial interests, England was calling upon the principle of *Mare Clausum* (closed sea), proposed by the scholar John Seldon, to justify its sovereignty over the waters surrounding their island. Seldon argued that the ancient Britons, the Romans, the Anglo-Saxons, the Normans, and the kings of England had consistently and successively dominated the ocean around England, as well as the island itself, and therefore had sovereignty over those seas.

Another aspect to consider is the principle of neutrality. In the history of nations that used the seas both to wage war and to transport trade goods, the idea of neutrality didn't even exist until about the end of the sixteenth century. Various European kings attempted to prevent merchant ships sailing from neutral countries from trading with the kings' enemies and claimed the right to seize such goods as well as the ships. In some periods, foreign vessels could enter only certain coastal harbors with produce from their own countries, not with material from trade with others. When, in the eighteenth century, the wealth of Europe began to grow because of increased traffic between the new American colonies and other trading countries, the maritime nations fought to gain supremacy and exclusivity on these watery highways. While major maritime powers such as France and England lost ships and men in these battles, other nations that, like Denmark, were neutral in relation to the major powers, filled the void in international trade by building their own merchant marines.

Two theories of law grew out of the historical confrontations between maritime powers seeking control of the seaways and neutral nations wanting to send their ships where and when they pleased. One theory says the high seas are *res nullius*—belonging to no one. The other says they are *res communis*—the property of everyone. But both theories attempt to draft some kind of law on which all nations can agree. The question was, and is, Where do the high seas begin? All coastal nations claim a "territorial sea" near their shores. The traditional claim was at one time about three nautical miles, since that was as far as most states could enforce their rights with shore cannon. But when President Harry Truman made claim for United States ownership of the continental shelf along its coasts in 1945, and then Chile, Ecuador, and Peru extended their coastal territorial seas to 200 miles in order to protect their fishing interests in 1952, the United Nations began holding meetings to discuss these legal questions. Conferences in Geneva held in 1958 and 1960 raised more questions than they answered, and the Third United Nations Law of the Sea Treaty Conference began in 1974 and concluded in 1982. There are certain basic questions the conference has tried to resolve. How far off its coastline does a nation have the territorial right to control access to its waters and the seabed beneath? Who has the right to resources of the oceans—both near coasts and in the high seas? Who has the right to navigate through straits? Who is responsible for the management of the living resources of the ocean? Who is responsible for protecting the oceans from pollution? Should scientific research in the ocean be totally free? Can there be international control of the high seas?

On April 30, 1982, one hundred thirty nations voted for the draft treaty at the United Nations; seventeen, including the Soviet

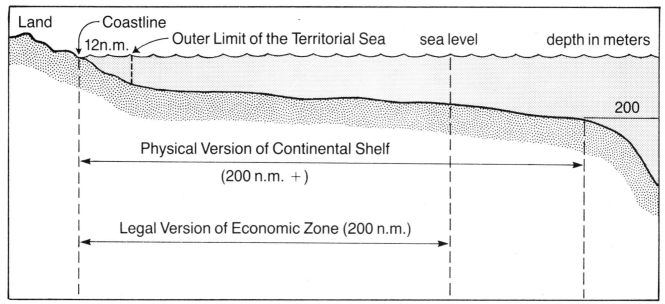

(A)

Land | Coastline
12n.m. | Outer Limit of the Territorial Sea | sea level | depth in meters

200

Physical Version of Continental Shelf
(200 n.m. +)

Legal Version of Economic Zone (200 n.m.)

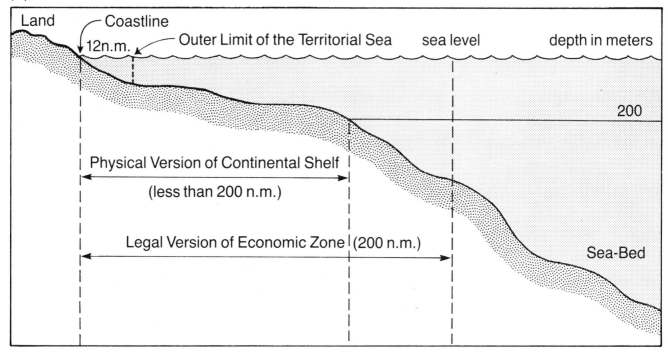

(B)

Land | Coastline
12n.m. | Outer Limit of the Territorial Sea | sea level | depth in meters

200

Physical Version of Continental Shelf
(less than 200 n.m.)

Legal Version of Economic Zone (200 n.m.)

Sea-Bed

The recent Law of the Sea Treaty Conference obtained agreement among the majority of nations on interpretations of territorial rights to coastal zones.

Union, abstained, and four, including the United States, voted no because they objected to some portions of the draft treaty. Those general guidelines that have been agreed on by most participating nations have expressed themselves in this draft treaty, subject to ratification by at least 60 nations to make it effective. The draft treaty covers navigation, coastal resources, the deep seabed, pollution, and freedom of scientific research. What are these guidelines?

First, most nations agree that the high seas should be free for passage by any ships, and the majority favor a twelve-mile territorial sea between coastal states and the beginning of the "high sea." This would create overlapping claims in some straits that are used for international traffic, but the treaty proposes that free right of transit for all ships and aircraft through or over such straits be permitted. Obligations as well as rights would be made subject to international traffic and antipollution controls.

Second, the world's most abundant fishing grounds are located within 200 miles from shore, as are 37 percent of the known oil reserves. Those factors have prompted the proposal for a 200-mile "exclusive economic zone" in which coastal states would have control while nonresource uses such as navigation and overflight would remain free to all. With that exclusive control would come responsibilities for the prevention of pollution and overfishing. Since some fish (like tuna) are highly migratory and cover vast distances through the waters of many nations, special international regulations have been incorporated into the treaty regarding both conservation of and harvesting rights to the tuna.

Third, with the discovery in the 1970s of the technology to recover mineral-rich manganese nodules from two and three miles down on the seabed floor, controversy arose among nations participating in the Treaty Conference. Those developing countries that do not have the mining technology to recover these minerals from the sea argue that since the high seas are the "common heritage of mankind," any profits from such exploitation should be

104

shared with all nations. They favor the establishment of an international seabed authority that would have access to privately developed technology. Those countries whose companies have spent large quantities of money developing the technology take the point of view that the deep seabed is clearly part of the high seas, so its resources are wide open to exploration by any nation with the desire and capability to do so. This is one aspect of the treaty that prompted President Reagan to instruct his delegates to the conference to vote against it, since the private developers in the United States would have to share their technology with developing nations through the international seabed authority.

Fourth, there are five major sources of ocean pollution, and the treaty attempts to deal with each of them. While some pollution derives from drilling on the continental shelf, from deep-seabed mining, from spills from vessels that traverse the seas, and from dumping of radioactive and other wastes, 90 percent of all marine pollution sources are land based. Pollutants seep into groundwater or are dumped into rivers that flow to the ocean. Polluting gases, hydrocarbons, and pesticides released into the atmosphere from factory stacks or spraying fall into the sea. The treaty presents international standards for acceptance to all nations in an effort to avoid the spoiling of the ocean environment so necessary to our lives.

Fifth, when an American marine scientist completes an experiment or a research exploration, he or she usually publishes the results in a scientific journal and the information is available to anyone in the world. The same situation applies with the scientists of many other nations. As oceanographic research has increased, however, some coastal nations say that freedom of scientific research primarily benefits the advanced countries. Since the 1958 Law of the Sea Convention, scientists are required to seek the prior consent of coastal nations before working anywhere on their continental shelves. Researchers say this places crippling restrictions on humankind's unending quest for knowledge, since in some cases permission has been denied arbitrarily or there has been no response to requests. An alternative has been proposed. Rather than having to seek prior consent, researchers would like to notify the coastal state in advance about the nature of research to be conducted, to invite nationals from the coastal state to participate, and to share the data with the host government. If the research were to be directly related to resources in a state's economic zone, the researchers wouldn't proceed without getting that state's consent.

There are 360 million cubic miles of water in the world's oceans, and almost every drop is a microcosmic world of life on this planet. Scientists are needed to help us understand how the life processes work and how to maintain the balance of the food chain so there is enough for all. We need to know how best to tap the energy sources of the oceans and how to preserve the beauty of a beach or a coral reef.

Comprehension of the scientific laws that rule the ocean and identification of the forces that threaten them is only half the battle. The other half is obtaining the commitment of all nations to weigh national self-interest against the best use of our planet. Treaties are an attempt to bridge such conflicts, but they are only as good as the will of the persons who sign them.

Negotiations are difficult because so many nations are involved, and each has its own interests to protect and advantages to seek. The most recent negotiations for a successful Law of the Sea Treaty have been under way for almost ten years. In December 1982, 117 nations signed the treaty, but forty-seven others opposed it or declined to vote. The treaty becomes law when the legislatures of sixty countries ratify it, and then it will become binding only on those that signed. It may take another decade to get all nations to agree on all the issues raised by the treaty, but the future of our oceans and our use of them depends upon such international cooperation.

BIBLIOGRAPHY

Anikouchine, Wm. A. and Richard W. Sternberg. *The World Ocean, An Introduction to Oceanography.* Englewood Cliffs, NJ: Prentice Hall, 1973.

Barton, Robert. *The Oceans.* New York: Facts on File, 1980.

Bassett, Fletcher S. *Legends and Superstitions of the Sea and of Sailors.* Detroit: Singing Tree Press, 1971.

Beiser, Arthur. *The Earth.* New York: Time-Life Books, 1971.

Bilang, Karla. *Voyages of Discovery, Through Artists' Eyes.* New York: St. Martin's Press, 1976.

Borgese, Elizabeth Mann. *Seafarm, The Story of Aquaculture.* New York: Harry N. Abrams, Inc., 1980.

Brittin, Burdick H. and Liselotte B. Watson. *International Law for Seagoing Officers.* 3rd edition. Annapolis: Naval Institute Press, 1972.

Carson, Rachel. *The Sea Around Us.* Revised edition. New York: New American Library, Inc., Signet Science Library Books, 1961.

Charlier, Roger Henri and Bernard Ludwig Gordon. *Ocean Resources: An Introduction to Economic Oceanography.* Washington, DC: University Press of America, Inc., 1978.

Cousteau, Jacques-Yves with James Dugan. *The Living Sea.* New York: Harper and Row, 1963.

Deacon, Margaret. *Scientists and the Sea, 1650–1900, A Study of Marine Science.* London: Academic Press, 1971.

Dubach, Harold W. and Robert W. Taber. *Questions About the Oceans.* Washington, DC: U.S. Naval Oceanographic Office, 1968.

Earle, Silvia A. and Al Giddings. *Exploring the Deep Frontier: The Adventure of Man in the Sea.* Washington, DC: National Geographic Society, 1980.

Engel, Leonard. *The Sea.* New York: Time-Life Books, 1970.

Gaskell, T.F. *World Beneath the Sea: The Story of Oceanography.* Garden City, NY: Natural History Press, 1964.

Groves, Donald G. and Lee M. Hunt. *The Ocean World Encyclopedia.* New York: McGraw-Hill, Inc., 1980.

Kulsrud, Carl J. *Maritime Neutrality to 1780.* Boston: Little Brown and Co., 1936.

Larson, David L. *Major Issues of the Law of the Sea.* Durham, NH: University of New Hampshire, 1976.

Leopold, Luna B., Kenneth S. Davis and the editors of *Life. Water.* New York: Time-Life Books, 1966.

Limburg, Peter. *Oceanographic Institutions.* New York: Thomas Nelson, Inc., 1979.

Marx, Wesley. *The Oceans: Our Last Resource.* San Francisco, CA: Sierra Club Books, 1981.

Matthews, Wm. H., III. *Invitation to Geology.* Garden City, NY: Natural History Press, 1971.

Mostert, Noel. *Supership.* New York: Warner Books, 1974.

Practising Law Institute. *Ocean and Coastal Law,* New York: Practising Law Institute, 1976.

Pinsel, Marc I. *150 Years of Service on the Seas, A Pictorial History of the U.S. Naval Oceanographic Office from 1830–1980,* (volume 1 1830–1946). Advance Edition. Bay St. Louis, MS: U.S. Naval Oceanographic Office, 1981.

Potter, Pitman B. *The Freedom of the Seas.* New York: Longmans, Green and Co., 1924.

Press, Frank and Raymond Siever, *Earth.* San Francisco, CA: W.H. Freeman, 1978.

Ross,David A. *Introduction to Oceanography.* New York: Meredith Corp., 1970.

Ross, David A. *Opportunities and Uses of the Ocean.* New York: Springer-Verlag, 1978.

Shepard, Francis P. *Geological Oceanography, Evolution of Coasts, Continental Margins, and the Deep-Sea Floor.* New York: Crane, Russak & Co., Inc., 1977.

Shepard, Birse. *Lore of the Wreckers.* Boston: Beacon Press, 1961.

Thurman, Harold. *Introductory Oceanography.* Columbus, OH: Charles E. Merrill Publishing Co., 1975.

University of Texas Petroleum Extension Services. *A Primer of Offshore Operations.* Austin, TX, 1976.

Voss, Gilbert L. *Oceanography.* New York: Golden Press, 1972.

Walsh, Don, ed. *The Law of the Sea.* New York: Praeger Publishers, 1977.

Warren, Bruce A. and Carl Wunsch, eds. *Evolution of Physical Oceanography.* Cambridge, MA: MIT Press, 1981.

Wilford, John Noble. *The Mapmakers: The Story of the Great Pioneers in Cartography—from Antiquity to the Space Age.* New York: Alfred A. Knopf, 1981.

Wooster, Warren S., ed. *Freedom of Oceanic Research.* New York: Crane, Russak & Co., Inc., 1973.

INDEX

flounder, 71
food chain, 66
Forbes, Edward, 53
fossils, 61
FPC (fish protein concentrate), 70
France, 15
Franklin, Benjamin, 13
Franklin's chart of the Gulf Stream, 14
freedom of oceanic research, 105

Galapagos Rift Zone, 54
gas from the sea, 44
Gehrig's Disease, Lou, 63
Geneva, 102
Genoese, 100
geologists, 28–30, 46, 54
Gibraltar, 15
Glomar Challenger, 31, 33–36
Glomar Explorer, 34
gold, 74–75
"greenhouse" effect, 83
Grotius, Hugo, 101
Gulf of Oman, 91
Gulf Stream, 13, 44
gyres, ocean, 13

haddock, 71
hatchetfish, 56
Hatteras, Cape, lighthouse, 18
Hawaii, 41
Hay, John, 92
heave compensator system, 36
Helios, 99
Henry II, 99
Henry VIII, 75
herbivores, 58
herring, 66
Hess, Harry, 12
High Pressure Nervous Syndrome, 22
high sea, 102
Himalayas, 30
Historia Animalium, 55

Iceland, 59
Indian Ocean, 9
Indonesia, 94, 97
Inter-Governmental Maritime Consultative Organization, 82
International Maritime Organization, 82, 94
International seabed authority, 105
International Whaling Commission, 59

iodine, 65
Irish moss, 72

jackup drilling rig, 46
Japan, 15, 50, 52, 59, 66–69, 72
Jaws (film), 58
Jessup, Keith, 75
jetsam, 99
Jim diving suit, 23
JOIDES (Joint Oceanographic Institutions for Deep Earth Sampling), 31

kelp, 44, 73
killer whale, 57
Korea, 59

Lafitte, Jean, 99
Lake Timsah, 93
Lamont-Doherty Geological Observatory, 35
Law of the Sea Treaty Conference, 37, 71, 80, 94, 95, 102, 103, 106
lead, 77
Lebanon, 91
Letter of Marque, 99
"library" of sediment drilling cores, 35
Ligurian Gulf, 100
limpet, 64
LNG (liquified natural gas), 44
load on top, 82
lobster, 56
London Dumping Convention, 83
Lusitania, 23

mackerel, 66
magnetometers, 46
Malacca Strait, 94, 96, 101
Malaysia, 94, 97
mammal, 58
manatees, 59
manganese nodules, 49
Mare Clausum, 101
Mare Liberum, 101
mariculture, 68
marine biologist, 22, 62
Maritime Administration, 96
marshes, 27
Mary Rose, 75
mathematicians and oceanography, 20
Mauna Kea, 26

Maury, Matthew, 20
Mediterranean, 12, 15, 34, 80, 90
mercenene, 63
merchant shipping, 20
mercury, 77
mermaids, 59
mesopelagic, 56
methane gas, 44
Mexico, 35
Mid-Oceanic Ridge, 26, 30
migratory species, 72
Minimata Bay, 77
Mississippi, 27
molybdenum, 49
moon, 9
Mount Everest, 26
Mount St. Helens, 26
"mud" engineer, 47
Mussel Watch, 79

National Science Foundation, 31
NATO (North Atlantic Treaty Organization), 90
nautical mile, 37
nautilus, 62
nekton, 56
Nelson, Lord, 15
neutrality, 101
nickel, 49, 77
Nimbus-7, 25
Niño, El, 66
Normans, 101
Norway, 59, 66

ocean bed, 28–29
ocean currents, 15, 16, 17
ocean formation, 12
ocean origin, 12
ocean ranching, 69
ocean size, 9
ocean thermal energy conversion (OTEC), 40–43
Oceans of the world (*illustration*), 10–11
oceans within oceans, 17
octopus, 56, 63
oil drilling rigs, 45, 46
oil formation, 45
oil spills, 80, 94
oil, undersea, 27
Outer Continental Shelf Lands Act, 38
overfishing, 71
oyster ranching, 68
oyster shells, 73

111